Warman's
Watches
FIELD GUIDE

D0734049

Dean Judy

Values and Identification

©2005 Dean Judy

Published by

kp books

An Imprint of F+W Publications

700 East State Street • Iola, WI 54990-0001
715-445-2214 • 888-457-2873

Our toll-free number to place an order or obtain
a free catalog is (800) 258-0929.

Library of Congress Catalog Number: 2004115471

ISBN: 0-89689-137-2

Designed by Jamie Griffin

Edited by Kristine Manty

Printed in United States of America

Contents

Introduction

Welcome to the fascinating world of vintage watch collecting. The search for, and collecting of, these miniature jeweled time machines is a wondrous journey full of fun, excitement, discovery, profit, and knowledge. In this field guide you will find a great cross-section of pocket watches and wrist watches from the 1870s to the 1970s.

What is a vintage watch? Generally speaking, anything made before 1960 is considered to be "vintage." Anything made before 1920 is considered to be "antique." I, however, don't subscribe to any strict lines of distinction and have chosen the arbitrary cutoff date to a "vintage" watch, as any watch that was made before the advent of the LCD (liquid crystal diode) quartz, battery powered, timepiece.

The quartz watch started taking over the market in the 1970s, but still there are some extremely collectible mechanical (wind-up) watches to be found from this decade, that are desirable. Quartz watches ruled the market after the '70s and still represent the vast majority of timepieces being produced today. The quartz watch, highly marketed early on by Texas Instruments and Seiko, nearly drove the Swiss watch industry to its knees, and took away the huge market share it had enjoyed for decades. Interestingly enough, it was the Swiss who invented the quartz technology, but at first they ignored it. Fortunately they regrouped, joined in, and saved themselves by coming out with watches like the "Swatch Watch." Today, the finest and most valuable watches are still produced in

Switzerland, and are mechanical (manual wind and automatic wind) timepieces, not quartz.

The later half of the 1800s and early part of the 1900s were high times for watch manufacturing, especially in America, and I consider watches from this period as vintage also. To me a "vintage" watch is one that can be worn and enjoyed, even if it is only on some special occasion. On the other hand, an "antique" watch is one I consider to be so fragile and old, it must remain at rest in a display case somewhere. The 100 years from the 1870s to the 1970s, the period of watch collecting that I love the best, took us from the "turnip" (large rounded pocket watch) to high-tech space age marvels worn on the wrist.

In this guide, we will review some history of watchmaking and collecting, tips on searching for watches, understanding how to ascertain the condition of vintage watches, buying and selling tips, values and prices, and a photo gallery of watches and memorabilia. For those of you just starting out in search of the vintage watch, I do hope this book will provide a spark that ignites a passion inside you to study, learn, and appreciate the wonderful world of horology, the study of the art and science of time, timekeeping, and timekeepers. For those seasoned watch lovers who are reading this, I do hope you find a helpful tip or two inside these pages, that may open up other avenues to your searching, and add to the pleasure of discovering just one more beautiful miniature machine.

Urban prospecting for the vintage watch

There are many ways to search for vintage timepieces, all of which I have not discovered yet, but I have had luck with the following ways:

Classified ads

Focusing your search can weed out the unwanted clunkers and cheaper "throw away" watches that come your way. In general, senior citizens have the lion's share of the vintage and antique watches that lie buried somewhere deep in an old sock drawer long forgotten. I run a continuous want ad in a small local "Senior News" newspaper that comes out monthly. The secret is to keep the ad running month after month and, as people come across their old watches, your ad will come to mind when they decide to part with it. Your ad might run like this: Watch collector seeks older mechanical (wind up) watches, working or not. Hamilton, Omega, Longines, Rolex, others. No Timex or Quartz. Please contact Bill Smith at 777-222-3333.

I have purchased many fine old timepieces from running ads like this one. I do, however, recommend that you get as much information over the phone as you can. When someone first calls, take the time to ask them a few important questions. Ask if their watch (or watches) is a wind-up type watch, if that is what you're looking for. Ask if they can tell you what brand or who the maker of the watch is. Are they all men's watches? Ladies' watches? Can they tell you approximately how old the pieces are? Can they describe the overall condition to you as average, fine, or near mint? If you feel you have a good rapport with the caller, you might find out how much they are asking for the watch, so you can bring the appropriate amount of cash with you. What you are trying to establish by asking these questions is if you are going on a wild goose chase or have a legitimate prospect.

Flea markets

Flea markets are another wonderful place to find old watches, and some of my best finds have come from these. I usually go around flea markets asking every person who is selling antiques or collectibles if they have brought any old watches with them that day. Many of these dealers and vendors keep the good stuff hidden out of sight and only bring it out if someone asks or seems interested. Don't forget to bring cards with you, with your name and number on them, to hand out to the dealers and vendors who left their "good watches" at home. Also, get there early. I cannot count the times when I've heard, "You're the fifth person to ask me about old watches this morning." Many times the regulars who sell at these marts keep watches they have come across in their travels between flea marts stashed away just to show to you when you come around, if it's one of the local affairs you frequent.

Also keep an eye out for vintage watch bands, watchcases, parts or pieces, for they don't take up much room, and they always come in handy at some point for restoration purposes or "trading stock" to other urban watch prospectors.

Thrift stores

Thrift stores, like the Salvation Army and Goodwill, are good places to check for vintage watches. At first, I was reluctant to go into these places because I figured all the good stuff was gleaned by the people in the back room or the members of the staff who went out and picked up the items at the collection points. However, old stuff attracts other old stuff, and sure enough, I have found good buys at these stores on occasion.

Garage sales

Of course, garage sales are also a great place for the intrepid urban prospector to find hidden treasures. If I don't see any older watches in a particular garage sale, I will always inform the person having the sale that I am interested in old-time, wind-up-type watches. Many times the people will have granddad's old railroad watch wrapped up in a sock somewhere in a dresser drawer. They won't even think to bring it out to a garage sale. Garage sale prices are also generally lower than flea market or thrift store prices.

Estate sales

I have found bargains at estate sales, when family and friends run the sale. But, as a rule, if professionals are hired, they are usually aware of vintage and antique watch values. However, sometimes when there is to be a huge estate sale and there is just too much stuff, an old watch may not be researched thoroughly and may be under-priced. Of course, being there early helps in finding any deals. If you contact the people who provide estate liquidation services, they can put you on their mailing list and keep you informed of upcoming estate sales where watches are present. They might even let you have the first look at them.

Auction houses

Live auctions are also a place to find old watches of value. Most towns and all cities have auctioneers who hold auctions regularly. If you decide to attend one, be sure to give yourself plenty of time to preview the items up for auction, prior to the sale. But always remember—knowledge is power. You have to do your due diligence and study the subject of watch collecting. If you can glance at a box full of watches and know the approximate retail value of a particular piece, and know it to be 10 times the starting bid price, that is power and you can use it accordingly.

Upscale auction houses, such as Sotheby's and Christie's, are knowledgeable of the current values of timepieces, and in many cases, set the values for the market. You get to see nicer pieces, but the prices are higher. I am not an expert in this area, but if money is not an issue, these upscale auction houses are wonderful places to view fabulous vintage watches. In the past, I have been on their mailing lists and have received beautiful color brochures and booklets describing upcoming auctions of fine timepieces. These make wonderful reference materials, even if you can't make the auctions.

Antiques shops

Antiques shops have been, for me, anyway, great places to find old watches. It is hard to be an expert in everything out there that is collectible or has value as an antique, and antiques dealers only know so much about everything in their shops. I have found many a good and fair deal in antiques shops and collectives. Antiques dealers also have connections with auctioneers, estate liquidators, junk dealers, and so on. If they know you are a serious buyer, they will keep their eyes open for you. Antiques collectives are an even greater resource for the urban prospector because there are so many dealers under one roof. In recent years, the cost of running an antiques store became too much for many dealers. So, dealers banded together to form collectives. They rented out different sized floor areas in their shops, and even rented out small glass showcase space. Some of these collectives are huge. There can be 50 different dealers selling merchandise in the same store and putting out old watches they've found.

The Internet

A person can spend days on the World Wide Web finding Web pages of people who deal in watches, auctions on watches, histories of watches, new watches, vintage watches, and so on. There are also chat rooms where you can learn more about watch collecting and perhaps make a contact to track down a special watch or part. One of the biggest boons to watch lovers is eBay. On any given day, you can find in excess of 35,000 watches up for auction on this Internet auction site.

The following are some tips I've discovered while trying to uncover cyber watch deals. It all boils down to the search. When you go to eBay and type the word "watch" in the search title, you will come up with approximately 30,000 to 35,000 watch auctions at any given time. This is where most sellers and buyers go. If you enter the word "wristwatch" in the search title, you will get only around 1,000 to 1,500 auctions that come up. Congratulations! You have just stepped ahead of thousands of other urban prospectors out there searching for deals. Most people just enter the one word "watch" in their search, kick back, and see what is out there. The same goes for "pocketwatch." If you separate the word into two words, i.e., "pocket watch," a lot more auctions will come up than if you just put in the one word. On eBay, the secret is to find auctions that few other watch prospectors have found. Also, the early bird gets the watches. Try searching for watch auctions that have just been recently listed, instead of the auctions just getting ready to end. You might be able to contact the seller and buy it early before 300 other vintage watch fans discover it.

eBay is not the only site on the Web to find vintage watches, so don't limit yourself. Sotheby's is a great place to discover beautiful watch auctions. It has a wide variety and you can always count on finding exotic and rare timepieces on its site. Christie's auction site is another wonderful place to visit for the urban prospector searching for treasures. When you are ready to locate the finest watches for your collection, consider contacting Antiquorum, world-class auctioneers of fine timepieces with offices in Geneva, Milan, Moscow, Paris, Hong Kong, New York, and Japan. Besides going to one of its auctions in person, you can also view and purchase watches online through its Internet Web site auctions.

The National Association of Watch and Clock Collectors

The National Association of Watch and Clock Collectors in Columbia, Pennsylvania, is an excellent organization to belong to and I highly recommend you join. The knowledge you gain and contacts made from being a member are well worth the low yearly dues you pay to join. The various chapters of the NAWCC have regular local meetings and special regional events all over the country, and overseas as well. The organization also has a great Internet site to visit at www.nawcc.org. Whether you attend local events, travel to regional meets, or read through its bi-monthly publications, the "NAWCC Bulletin" and the "Mart," your horological world will be enhanced immeasurably. The NAWCC also has The National Watch & Clock Museum and a library and research center.

American Watchmakers-Clockmakers Institute

The American Watchmakers-Clockmakers Institute in Harrison, Ohio, is a not-for-profit trade association for watchmakers and clockmakers. AWI is dedicated to the advancement of its members and their professions through educational and technical services. You do not have to be a watchmaker to join the AWI. It is a great association for those interested in the restoration aspect of watch collecting. The AWI has an informative monthly publication, "The Horological Times," which contains features written by recognized experts dealing with the techniques of servicing and repairing watches, clocks, and the functional characteristics of mechanical, electronic, and antique timepieces. This, combined with a large classified ad section and regular watch industry news, provides a great resource for all horologists. The AWI also has a movement bank/material search network. The American Watchmakers-Clockmakers Institute is the place to start for anyone who is considering becoming a watchmaker or repair person. They have an Academy of Watchmaking, bench courses, and a certification program.

I am a member of AWI and highly recommend the association. It is the perfect source for locating watchmakers in your area and tracking down parts and information. The AWI has an educational library and a museum. You can visit its great Web site, too, at www.awi-net.org.

Condition, condition, condition

At some point after you have made the decision to become an urban prospector and search for watch treasure, you will need to acquire a few basic "tools of the trade." When I'm out urban prospecting, I always carry my small "watch inspection kit" in a belt pouch that contains the following items: One good pair of tweezers, one rubber vacuum case opener for pocket watch (screw back) cases, one watchcase opening knife (for wrist and pocket watches), one decent loupe for magnification, and a few small plastic Zip-lock bags to place the timepieces I find in. Armed with these few tools, a person can inspect most pre-1960 timepieces.

Now you are ready to check out your first stash of newly acquired watches. Get a feel for handling them, holding them, and inspecting their tops and bottoms, sides and ends. At this point, you can start to develop your "extra sensory perception" while attempting to understand what this little machine went through while strapped on the wrist of, or bounced around in the pocket of, its previous owner. Use all of your senses—this will come in handy when out in the field—and look at the overall condition of the watch. Did its owner take good care of it? Was it abused, thrashed, crashed, scratched, and dropped? Is it ticking? Is it tocking? Is it humming? Is it silent? Does it rattle? Does it have apparent moisture inside the crystal? All of this early experience will come in handy when you go out into the "real" world and begin your urban prospecting. Go ahead and start grading them on a scale of 1 to 10 (10 being the highest). This is good practice for when you are out

Before: Gruen, circa 1960s, in as-found condition, with a broken crystal and dirty case.

After: Gruen, Precision-auto wind, circa 1960s, after crystal replacement and case cleaned.

A 1940s' Swiss-made Gubelin in as-found condition.

in the field, since you will need to access the condition of timepieces quickly, and occasionally not under the best circumstances—inadequate lighting, minimal tools available for inspection, time constraints, etc. After checking out as many watches as you have on hand at home, you will be ready to go out buying in the field.

It has been said that the three most important things to consider when buying, selling, or appraising real estate are "location, location, location." Well, where vintage watches are concerned, you can say "condition, condition, condition" as being the most important considerations. When you are contemplating buying a watch, you must ask yourself over and over, "What is the true state that this timepiece is in, at present?" You must study the watch closely and ascertain its accurate condition. Is it in average condition? Is it in mint condition? How do I tell?

Visual and mechanical condition

When you examine a watch, look at the dial (the face), and get a feel for what the watch has been through. Ask questions from the owner and try to learn the history of the piece. Let the watch "speak to you." A fellow watch fanatic, collector, dealer, buyer, seller, friend of mine, once said when I showed him one I had for sale, "The watch just doesn't speak to me." He is so right in thinking this way. You need to reach out with your sixth sense sometimes when contemplating buying a watch and get the feel of it. This is especially true if you're going to be bidding on one, or you need to make a quick decision when in a buying situation. Or, when you are on "the excitement plan" with your credit card in hand, eyes glazed over with anticipation, and your heart is beating way over 9,000 rpm! Remember, it is very easy to buy a watch, but sometimes it can be very hard to resell it, especially if you bought high (high price and high on the idea of owning it), or didn't eyeball it closely.

What does the dial say? If your sixth sense is foggy, then tune up your other five senses to examine the watch. Is the dial an original one? This is of utmost importance to collectors, for in the past it was a common practice for watchmakers to send the dial off to be refinished, if it had even a little wear, when the watch came in for a service. The watchmaker made a little extra money and the customer now had a watch that looked brand new when they came to pick it up. If it's a Swiss watch,

A 1940s' Gubelin with crystal removed.

does it say "Switzerland," "Swiss," or "Swiss Made" on the bottom of the dial? Does the dial have any stains, discoloration, cracks, chips, scratches, dings, or dents? Is the paint faded or partly missing? If the dial is enamel, does it have any hairline cracks that can be seen with the naked eye or under magnification? If the dial has been restored in the past and is not the original, how does the refinish work look? Was it a quality refinish job? Is it crisp? Lines straight and wording correct?

Move next to the hands. Are they straight? Do the hands match and are they original? Look at the center where the hands attach. Is it all scratched up in the center of the hands? Do they look like they have been taken off and put back on 50 times? Examine the crown. Does it look to be an original one, or does it have the watch manufacturer's logo or name on it? Does it sit up against the body of the case straight and close? Does it wobble out of round when you turn it (bent stem or crown tube)? Turn the crown. What does it feel like? Is it a smooth winding feel? When winding the mainspring does it skip or feel scratchy (winding mechanism wheels or pinion teeth problems)? Do you wind and wind and wind but never seem to get it fully wound (mainspring broken or slipping)? Pull the crown out into the setting position. Does it stay pulled out smartly, or slip back in (broken setting bridge)? Now turn the crown for setting the hands and notice how it feels.

Gubelin, circa 1940s, refinished/restored, stainless steel, dial refinished but hands kept in original condition.

Is it hard to turn the crown or does it turn too freely (too tight or too loose cannon pinion)? Do the hands line up correctly? Do the hands hit the dial or touch the roof of the crystal? What condition is the crystal in? Is it plastic or glass? Tap it on your front teeth. With practice, you can tell the difference between the two. Plastic crystals can usually have their scratches all polished out. Glass ones are harder to restore when all scratched and chipped. Any cracks or breaks in the crystal will allow moisture and dust inside the dial area, and will need to be replaced.

Next, check out the case. Does it look original to the movement? What material is it made from? Solid gold, gold filled, gold plated, platinum, silver, nickel silver, stainless steel, chrome-plated base metal? Visually, what condition is it in? Note any wear through the plating, or brass showing through; notice any dents, dings, scratches, pitting, bent, or misshapen areas. If it is a pocket watch with a threaded back and bezel, are they cross-threaded or do they screw on and off smoothly? If the case has a snap fit bezel and back, check for scratches and marring that an errant case opener knife left. If it is a hunter case pocket watch, check to see if the bezel is in place and is the correct one. If

A "hacker" attempt at watch repair ruined this fine old Howard. Note the upper right-hand corner.

A 1930's Bulova with badly
rusted hands and dial.

The same 1930's Bulova,
with dial restored and hands
replaced, **$95-$195**.

you are examining a wrist watch case, look to see if the fits are close
between the body and bezel, and the back and body. Check to see if
the lugs are straight.

If it is a runner, listen to the movement. Does it sound strong
and steady no matter what position you hold it in? Is the movement
loose inside the case—does it rattle? If it is an automatic winding-
type watch, can you hear the rotor when it spins around? Is it a
smooth sound or can you hear the rotor hitting the case back or the
movement plate? If the watch is a complicated one, have the owner
show you the different functions and how they work. Ask the seller
if it is OK to open the back up and visibly check out the movement
if possible. If you are able to get that far into the watch, look on the
underside of the case back for screw head marks where movement

case screws may have backed out and worn into the case. Also look under the case back for watchmaker marks, as they can tell you a story of how often the movement was serviced through the years.

Inspect the condition of the movement and look for rust spots, especially on the hairspring. Examine the balance wheel area. Does the balance wheel turn freely and smoothly? Does it wobble? Look closely at the screw heads holding the movement together. Look at the slots in the screw heads where the screwdriver blade fits. Are they all in good shape, or have they been marked up by being removed and replaced too many times by careless repair people? There are a lot of "hackers" out in the watch world, who, after reading a couple

A 1920s' Gelbros, with broken crystal.

The same Gelbros Swiss, with fancy engraved case, radium hands, and glass crystal replaced, **$100-$200**.

A damaged 1890's enamel pocket watch dial.

The same enamel pocket watch dial, after the author repaired the damaged areas.

of repair manuals and looking at a few pictures, believe that they are master watchmakers. I have opened many a fine watch to sadly see screwdriver skid marks across a bridge or plate, and screw heads broken and messed up.

Many watch collectors are only interested in the outward appearance of their vintage watch. Whether it functions properly mechanically or not is a secondary consideration. I must say that the condition of the outward appearance is probably the most important factor in most peoples' minds, but you should get in the habit of grading the watch as a whole. If you have not yet established a relationship with a qualified watch repair person, seek one out as soon as possible. Once you have found a competent watchmaker to work with, he or she will assist you in keeping your vintage watches in top condition. Contact the American Watchmakers-Clockmakers Institute for help in finding a watchmaker in your area.

When buying a watch, you can use the rating scale on page 24 to help place a value on the timepiece.

10. Positively mint	NOS, unused, factory fresh, and still in the original box.
9. Mint +	Pristine, in original box, perhaps slightly or rarely used, but looks as if it was never used.
8. Mint	In original condition with only little use and no scratches, marks or wear.
7. Near mint	In original condition, used but with only faint marks or wear.
6. Fine +	Taken very good care of, with original parts used in any repairs or restoration. Little scratches, marks, or wear.
5. Fine	Crisp with only minor wear, marks, and scratches. Still has original case, dial may have had quality restoration done, has original movement.
4. Average	Wear from normal use for its age, but still with original case, dial (may have been refinished), and movement. Normal dings, wear marks, and scratches expected from daily use.
3. Fair	Well used, and may not have the original case, dial, or movement.
2. Poor	Broken, not working, parts missing, well worn, but restorable.
1. Junk	Totally worn out, damaged, rust, parts watch only.

Restoration

When you find a vintage watch worthy of restoration, you must consider all of what that entails. Let us say that you discover a wrist watch in 4 grade (average) condition, with a badly discolored dial. To restore the dial or not to restore the dial, that is the question.

Generally speaking, a dial has to be fairly well gone before I refinish it. Collectors always prefer a watch with an original dial. However, if it is just plain ugly, then get it refinished. Sometimes it is a tough call and a lot of the decision rests with what you plan to do with the watch after restoration. If you enjoy the look of the watch and plan to wear it, then getting the dial redone is a question of personal preference. If you obtained the watch with the desire to resell it, then you might consider cleaning up the case, crystal, and movement, but leave the decision to restore the dial to the next owner. However, if the dial is too ugly, there might not be a next owner anytime soon.

You must be careful and examine the dial closely to see if it will stand up to a light cleaning. Your watchmaker will know best what to recommend as far as dial cleaning goes. Usually you're better off not trying to clean it. Enamel dials are easier to have cleaned, as the enamel has been kiln fired onto metal and the lettering and numbers are more stable. Repairs can also be made on enamel dials, but keep in mind that enamel is like glass and you must be careful with them. Hairline cracks can grow and chunks can fall off if these dials are mistreated. A huge percent of vintage wrist and pocket watches with enamel dials have pronounced or faint hairline cracks in them. It is exciting to find one of these fine old watches with a perfect dial on it. Enamel dials with hairlines can be placed in an "ultrasonic cleaner" and the hairlines will disappear. However, they will return as soon as dust and dirt starts settling in the cracks again. Examine them closely with a good loupe to determine if they are free of hairlines or not.

Many times, a watch just needs a good polish and a new crystal to look new again. To restore vintage watchcases, there are watchcase repair experts that can re-plate gold-plated cases, repair broken hinges, make new bezels, fix holes, dings, and deep scratches. Solid gold cases are easier to polish up and restore than gold plated or gold-filled ones. Gold-filled cases are the next best thing to solid gold (gold filled is like an Oreo cookie lying on its side; there is

A 1950's Bulova with a badly discolored dial.

The restored Bulova, gold filled, diamond dial, after dial restoration, **$95-$195**.

base metal inside, usually brass, with thick plates of gold on the outsides). In the past, pocket watchcases were sometimes marked "5 Years," "10 Years," "Warranted 20 Years," etc. This is an indication of how thick the gold plates were when the case was made. Can you imagine anything warranted for 20 years nowadays? It's amazing that these gold-filled cases were made so well that the manufacturer could guarantee they would hold up for 10 or 20 years. Actually, most of these vintage gold-filled cases lasted many times longer than their warranty before any of the gold wore off to reveal the brass sandwiched inside. Rolled gold plate, sometimes stamped on cases as R.G.P., is the same as gold-fill, except the gold plating is thinner than gold-filled cases. The R.G.P. watchcases did not hold up as long as the gold filled ones, but would last better than the next category, which is the gold-electroplated case. These cases just have a few microns of gold plating. Great care has to be used when polishing and restoring them to original finish.

Restoration of gold filled and rolled gold-plated cases is tricky business. On wrist watchcases, the sharp edges usually wear through first—the corners, high spots, edges of the bezel and back, under the lugs, and also the tips of the lugs are the first to go. The case repairer must solder and/or re-plate the case. Depending on the severity of the wear, many times it just isn't worth the time and money to fully restore a badly worn-through gold-filled or R.G.P. case.

Restoring the movement of a vintage watch depends on the age of the timepiece and availability of parts. If the movement just needs a cleaning and oiling, this is to be considered standard maintenance. If the movement has broken or rusted parts, you will need an estimate for repair and restoration from a competent watchmaker or repair person. Watches manufactured prior to the 1950s might not be shock protected and must be examined for balance staff problems. If it was manufactured prior to the 1940s, it definitely wasn't shock protected, since few watches had this feature prior to that time. When a watch is dropped or shocked severely, the balance staff and the crystal are the first to break. When examining a watch, see that the balance turns while the watch is held in various positions. A watch with a broken balance staff may work in one position, but not in another. A watch that is old, or one that is rare where only a few were originally made or have survived, can usually have parts made for it if none are available. This is most always an expensive and time-consuming process.

Suffice it to say that the more you inspect and handle these little machines, the better you will become at knowing what to look for, and the better you will become at judging their true condition, condition, condition.

Buying and selling

First, let me warn you right now of the problem of fakes in the market. Most of us have seen the cheap fake Rolex watches that are out there by the millions. If you are not sure how a fake Rolex measures up to the real McCoy, go to your local Rolex dealer and ask to see a few.

Fake Rolexes hurt dealers' businesses and I'm sure they wouldn't mind letting you handle a couple. That way, you can get the feel and heft, and notice the craftsmanship and attention to detail that goes into making each one. Newer fakes are easy to spot once you have spent the time checking out the real thing.

However, now that I've said that, a friend of mine, in his travels, came across a fake made to look exactly like a 1940s vintage Rolex. These are hard for the rookie to identify and you must be careful. Always buy from a reputable dealer and remember to pay attention to detail and workmanship when inspecting the piece. There are some really good fakes of Omega watches out there and I myself was nearly fooled by one until I removed the back to inspect the movement. The outside of the watch, including the dial, looked authentic and the finish was relatively crisp. Once I peeked in the back, though, I knew it was fake. Be careful you don't get stung.

Buying

If you are just starting to collect vintage watches, it is a good idea to concentrate on just one kind of watch: American 21-jewel pocket watches or automatic-wind wrist watches, or just one brand/maker of watches, such as Hamilton, Waltham, Longines, Omega, Gruen, Mido, Vacheron Constantin, etc. This way, you can become fairly knowledgeable about your particular favorite watches in a relatively short amount of time. In my early collecting days, I would buy anything and everything as long as I thought I was getting a deal. After ending up with drawers full of every kind of watch, in every kind of condition (mostly broken), I decided to be a little pickier. If you run into good deals on watches that are not the kind

An example of an early cylinder-type escapement.

An example of modern lever escapement.

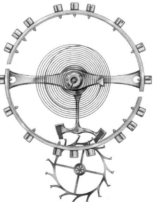

you collect, you can always use them for "trading stock" to other dealers or watchmakers, who are always looking for parts. Just be careful not to buy everything you come across or you can spend a lot of money and not have as much to show for it. It is a far better investment to buy a couple mint or near mint timepieces than two dozen below-average-condition clunkers.

When you have discovered a watch you want, you must truthfully ask yourself a few questions. How you answer these questions will help you decide how much you're willing to spend on any given watch. What are you buying the watch for? Are you going to keep it and add the piece to your collection? Are you going to resell the watch? If you are going to sell it, are you going to sell it at a wholesale price or a retail price?

When you ask the seller how much they want for the watch and they say, "I was hoping you could tell me what it is worth," you will have to do some quick calculations in your head. If you are going to keep the watch for your own collection, you can pay a little more for it, as you don't have to think about turning a profit. If you plan to resell it, it is good to remember to "buy low and sell high." Until I really studied the market, I used to "buy high and sell low." Then I discovered it was more fun the other way. Knowledge is the key.

When you are speaking to someone on the phone about a watch and, after finding out what kind it is (gent's, lady's) and who the maker is, here are some questions to ask:

1. Does the watch wind up and does it run? Can you pull the crown (winder) out and set the hands?

2. What color is the dial (face) and what condition is it in? Is it the original dial or has it been restored/refinished at some point in the past? What is written (printed) on the dial? If it is a Swiss watch, it should have "Swiss," "Swiss Made," or "Switzerland" printed at the bottom of the dial, below the six o'clock position.

3. What material is the case made of—stainless steel, yellow gold, white gold, gold filled, rolled gold plate, gold electroplate, silver, nickel, chrome plate?

4. What condition is the case in? Any dents? Dings? Scratches? Worn spots? Is there any engraving on the watch?

5. What is the history of the piece?

6. How would the overall condition and appearance of the watch be rated? Average? Fine? Mint?

7. What is the asking price?

You will soon get a feel for the person you are talking to, and for the watch they're selling. Listen closely and try to picture the piece in your mind as they describe it to you.

The following are a few tips for making an offer on a vintage watch. This part of the process can be an art in itself. You can get people mad at you, embarrass yourself to no end, and help create some bad vibes if you don't proceed with caution. If you are at an auction or an antiques shop where the price is already fixed, you cannot expect to do much bargaining. However, if you are buying over the phone from an ad you placed, or at a flea market, garage sale, or estate sale, you might be able to negotiate the price. If I ask the seller how much they want for the watch and they say they don't know and ask me what it's worth, I tell them exactly what I know to be true.

Let's say, for instance, it is a circa early 1960s stainless steel Omega "Seamaster" automatic-wind wrist watch that needs servicing, as it has sat in a drawer for 20 years. You have judged the watch to be in the #6, Fine + condition. In this scenario, the watch is working OK and doesn't need any parts; it just needs a cleaning,

An example of
Swiss chronograph
movement.

oiling, and polishing. In this case, I will tell them their watch, when serviced and in excellent running condition, is worth around $295 to a collector. But I also tell them I have to put some time, effort, and money into the piece to bring it up to standard, and then will have to search out a collector who loves the watch enough to part with $295 for it. Since we also live in good old capitalist America, I also note I need to make a little profit for my efforts and can therefore offer them $125 for their watch. After I explain this to the person, nine times out of 10 they say they understand I've got to make a little something on the deal and my offer sounds like a fair price.

What to buy?

So, what's hot? Generally, as for wrist watches, I believe you can never go wrong by picking up good quality stainless steel men's pieces, especially brand name automatic-wind wrist watches. Unusually shaped wrist watches, watches with complications (day, date, chronograph functions, moonphase, alarm, world time, repeater, etc.), limited edition pieces (watches the factory didn't make many of), early wrist watches from the 1910s and 1920s, and rose gold (pink gold) wrist watches are your best bets. Stainless steel wrist watches from the 1940s through the 1960s seem to be real hot collectibles. As for pocket watches, look for early examples of the top American and Swiss makers (low serial numbers), American railroad grade and railroad approved 10- and 18-size pocket watches, hunter case watches, pocket watches with multicolored dials, and high-grade Swiss pocket watches, especially ones made in the 1960s and 1970s, which are rather hard to find.

As for ladies' watches, what is highly collectible seems to be wide open for debate. At present, tiny ladies' watches from the 1940s through the 1960s do not seem to be highly sought after, and larger watches have become more popular with ladies now. Higher grade, name brand, women's wrist watches such as Movado, Longines, Omega, Rolex, Cartier, Vacheron Constantin, etc. are always popular no matter what size, especially if they are unusual in some way or have diamonds or other stones set into their cases. I like early (larger pieces) 1910s or 1920s Elgin, Hamilton, and Gruen ladies' watches, especially if they have enamel on them.

Ladies' pocket watches and pendant watches are a bit fragile and rather high-maintenance items, if you are going to bounce them around in everyday use. For this reason, I don't see a huge interest in this area. Still, the enamel ladies' pieces are little works of art and are sought after for their beauty. The whole area of collectible ladies' watches is a huge market waiting to catch fire. It seems that men are the biggest collectors of watches and have been for some time. I would love to see more women get excited about collecting the smaller timepieces, as they are truly marvels of miniature engineering, craftsmanship, and beauty. The watch factories across the world have, since they began mass production, employed thousands of women to assemble the watches. It is high time the ladies started buying back, and collecting, what they themselves helped to create.

Selling

The following are some points to consider if you want to sell a watch. Are you going to guarantee the watch or are you going to use the old flea-market rule of "20 seconds or 20 feet?" In other words, you'll only guarantee the piece for 20 seconds after the buyer purchases it or until the buyer gets 20 feet away from you with it; after that, they're on their own. If you use this rule, you will need to inform potential buyers that perhaps the watch has been lying in an old drawer for 42 years and, although it might tick for a bit, it isn't going to tock and you are not guaranteeing it to keep good time. Inform the buyer they should consider having it serviced should they want to wear it; or, in the case of pocket watches, carry it. If you have spent time and money going through the watch and have it all polished and running great, let the buyer know this also. Explain to them all that was done to the timepiece—overhaul, services, parts replaces, etc. If you have had the watch fully serviced and can now guarantee it to run and keep time, the selling price should reflect this. Some collectors would rather take care of the servicing on their own (they do it themselves or take it to their trusted watchmaker), as this is part of their excitement and collecting fun.

Where do you go to sell your watch?

As a rule, collectors pay the highest prices for watches. They are going to keep the watches they purchase and don't have to worry so much about saving room for profit when buying them. Watch dealers, of course, need to buy low and sell high to stay in business; therefore, you won't generally get as much for your watches from them. However, you might sit on your watch for a long time waiting to find the right collector to come by and fall in love with it. Dealers are in touch with many collectors and you might be able to turn your watches over faster through them.

To sell watches, you need to go where the dealers and collectors go: the Internet, AWI, NAWCC, antiques shops, antiques shows, auction houses, networking, advertising, etc. You can rent a space in an antiques collective to display and sell your timepieces. Most of these collectives rent space in their showcases and are perfect spots for selling small items like watches. You can also offer your items to dealers who already have showcase spots set up with watches. Joining the AWI and the NAWCC, and attending local and regional shows are excellent avenues for selling watches. Plus, it's a lot of fun.

The Internet is a great avenue for selling your watches, since you are placing them in front of hundreds and maybe even thousands of watch lovers and potential buyers. You can join an online auction service and in no time at all conduct your own watch auctions. There are also many Web sites set up by vintage watch dealers and you can contact them directly about selling your timepieces, as they are always looking to acquire more items for their businesses. Many times these dealers are also into the watch repair business, and so you can offer them watches that are not running or that need restoration. You can list your watches online with big auction houses such as Sotheby's, if you don't mind paying them a percentage of the sale. Antiquorum is a wonderful auction service, as it specializes in fine timepieces, and is one of the world's leading auctioneers in the field of horology. If you want to display and sell watches from your collection, you can look into setting up your own vintage watch Web site. There are Web-based "chat rooms" for sharing information, too.

I have successfully sold hundreds and hundreds of watches over the years through NAWCC, setting up spots in collectives, and on the Internet. Wherever you go to sell your watches, remember this: Always describe the watch accurately and truthfully. Don't sell any hidden surprises to people. If you don't know everything about a piece, then tell prospective buyers that. Point out any known flaws so the buyer knows exactly what they're buying. The golden rule applies here. The reward in doing this is obvious—people appreciate the honesty and they will become repeat customers.

Watch values and identification

If you think you have a valuable vintage watch in your possession and want to know its value, then you must gather knowledge about it. This book is meant to be a guide for you in the search for answers to the question of "What is the current market value of my watch?" The key word here is "guide." This guide is not the last word on the value of watches, and it is not meant to be the complete "watch bible and encyclopedia" on the subject. I have endeavored to give you a snapshot slice of the world of watches.

As Rene Rondeau says in his book, *Hamilton Wristwatches: A Collector's Guide*, "Watch prices are at best a moving target." The values of vintage watches change with trends in the market, the state of our economy, tastes in personal attire, what era in time happens to be cool and trendy this season, etc. All I do know is that values of vintage watches have done nothing but go up in the past two decades, and I don't see it slowing down.

The watch prices listed in this guide are for watches in good running condition, with all parts in place, band and crystal, etc., and are, for the most part, retail prices. They are prices that one would expect to pay in a retail environment like an antiques shop, vintage/estate jewelry establishment, professional watch dealer, or fine auction house. I have listed price ranges of watches in average to near mint condition. If your watch is in need of repairs or is in less than average condition, the value of the timepiece will be less than the average price, to reflect some of the cost of repairs and restoration. If the watch in question is in mint condition, then the sky is the limit and you can name your price. The limiting factors are condition, rarity, and demand.

Here is a small list of the names of watches and watch manufacturers, to keep your prospector's eye out for: Agassiz, Alpina, Angelus, Assmann, Audemars Piguet, Ball Watch Co., Baume & Mercier, J.W. Benson, Benrus, Blancpain, Breguet, Breitling, Bucherer, Bulova, Cartier, Chopard, Columbus Watch Co., Croton, Cyma, Dent, Ditisheim, Doxa, Ebel, Eberhard, Ekegren, Elgin, Eterna, Favre Leuba, Gallet, Geneve, Girard Perregaux, Glasshutte, Glycine, Goering, Golay, Gotham, Gruen, Gubelin, Hafis, Hamilton, Hampden, Harwood, Hebdomas, Helbros, Heuer, E. Howard & Co., E. Howard Watch Co. (Keystone), Huguenin, Illinois Watch Co., Ingersoll, E. Ingraham Co., International Watch Co., Junghans, Jules Jurgensen, Juvenia, Lancaster Watch Co., A. Lange & Sohne, Le Coultre, Lemania, Longines, Lucien Piccard, C. H. Meylan, Mido, Minerva, Montbrillant, Moser Cie., Movado, Ulysse Nardin, New England Watch Co., New Haven, New York Standard, Nivada, Non-Magnetic Watch Co., Ollendorf, Omega, Patek Philippe, Patria, Piaget, Pierce,

Pulsar, Rado, Record, Roamer, Rockford Watch Co., Rolex, Roskopf, Rotary, Sandoz, Seiko, Seth Thomas, Shreve & Co., South Bend Watch Co., Tavannes, Tiffany & Co., Tissot, Trenton Watch Co., Universal, United States Watch Co., Vacheron Constantin, Vulcain, Wakmann, Waltham Watch Co. (American Waltham Watch Co.), Waterbury Watch Co., Westclox, Wittnauer, Wyler, Zenith, and Zodiac.

These are all watches I have run across at some point in my 26-year journey. There are many more names out there and too many to list. If a business, or even an individual, wanted to have their name placed on the dial of a watch, and if they placed a large enough order with the watch manufacturer, one could have anything printed on the dial. So it is that there are many watches to be found with jeweler's names, etc., printed on the dial. The following watches are but a sampling of the millions and millions that are out there waiting to be discovered.

Abbreviations used:

GF = Gold filled	LS = Lever set
GP = Gold plated	OF = Open face
HC = Hunter case	PS = Pin set
J = Jewel	RR = Railroad

Pocket Watches

Many early watch manufacturers decorated their watch dials and cases with locomotives and other railroad scenes. This, however, does not denote them to be true railroad grade or railroad-approved timepieces. Railroad standards were implemented in the 1890s and had nothing to do with the decoration on the case or the dial of the watch.

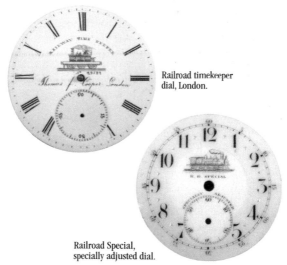

Railroad timekeeper dial, London.

Railroad Special, specially adjusted dial.

Pocket watch case, back engraved early train.

Pocket watch with red numbers and train.

Gold pocket
watch with train.

Senate Express train.

White dial with train, Swiss.

Railroad timekeeper dial, English.

Swiss train dial watch regulator.

Railway timekeeper dial.

Swiss watch, railroad
train dial.

Swiss, 1900s nickel case
engraved with Swiss cross
with wings, wheel on
earth. Railroad logo.

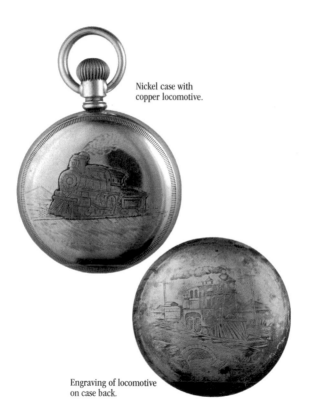

Nickel case with
copper locomotive.

Engraving of locomotive
on case back.

Agassiz Watch Co., circa 1920, 21J 43mm nickel case, power reserve indicator, center seconds stop/start feature, **$2,000-$2,500.**

Photo courtesy of Antiquorum.

Agassiz, World Time, circa 1945, 14k, **$5,000-$7,000.**

Photo courtesy of Antiquorum.

Agassiz movement view.

Agassiz, 17 ligne Swiss chronograph, 14k, **$1,500-$2,000.**

Auroa Watch Co.
Movement.

Aurora Watch Co.,
circa 1884, first-
year production,
GF 18 size 15J OF,
$295-$495.

Ball Watch Co., Cleveland, Ohio

Founded in the early 1890s by Webb C. Ball. Famous for its marketing of high-grade railroad watches produced by companies such as Elgin, Hamilton, Illinois, and Waltham. The company's pocket watches are highly prized by collectors today.

Ball, 16 size official railroad standard, 21J RR, GF case, **$400-$900.**

Ball dial, commercial standard (Swiss), 16 size, dial only, **$50-$150.**

Ball 999B, circa 1900s, 21J 16 size, **$695-$1,195.**

Columbus Watch Co., Columbus, Ohio

Founded in 1882 and sold in 1903 to establish the South Bend Watch Co. in Indiana.

Columbus, 18 size, 16J Railway King movement.

Columbus, Railway King, circa 1899, 18 size 16J Railway King movement, nickel case-Sidewinder, **$300-$600.**

Columbus movement.

Columbus, Railway King, circa 1899, GF HC with Railway King dial, 16J, **$300-$600.**

Dudley Watch Co.

Started in the early 1920s, this company of Lancaster, Pennsylvania, produced a limited number of pocket watches in which the bridges took the form of Masonic symbols.

Dudley Masonic movement, serial #5858.

Dudley Masonic, circa late 1940s, 12 size, third model, display back, YGF, **$1,500-$2,500.**

Elgin (Elgin National Watch Co.), Elgin, Illinois

Founded in 1864, this company produced more jeweled watches than any other in America during its more than 90-year history. The company made low-end watches, all the way up through to its famous high-quality railroad grades. These railroad pocket watches are highly sought after, as is the company's very collectible Art Deco wrist watches.

Elgin, Veritas 21 J RR movement.

Elgin, Veritas, circa 1901, dual time zone, sterling 21J 18 size, **$395-$795.**

Elgin, Veritas case.

Elgin/BW Raymond, 18 size 19J movement.

Elgin, BW Raymond, circa 1908, 19J 18 size, GF case, double sunk dial, **$175-$375.**

Elgin, circa 1910, 18 size 17J HC, diamond,
sapphire, and ruby, **$3,000-$3,500.**

Photo courtesy of Antiquorum.

Elgin, circa 1908,
15J nickel, 18 size,
$125-$225.

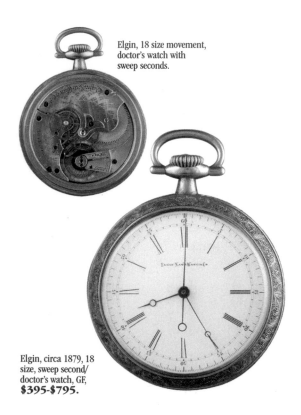

Elgin, 18 size movement, doctor's watch with sweep seconds.

Elgin, circa 1879, 18 size, sweep second/ doctor's watch, GF, **$395-$795.**

Elgin, three-finger bridge movement, Grade 270.

Elgin RR, circa 1902, grade 270/three-finger bridge, 21J 16 size, nickel case, **$295-$495.**

Elgin, BW Raymond
#571, 21J movement.

Elgin, BW Raymond
RR, #571, circa 1940,
16 size, GF, 21J 9 adj.,
$200-$500.

Elgin, 16S, 17J grade,
574 movement.

Elgin, circa 1950,
16 size 17J, GF OF,
$195-$395.

Elgin, 21J, three-finger bridge, high-grade movement #156.

Elgin, circa 1896, 21J
16 size, 14kt fancy HC,
$595-$1,095.

Elgin, BW Raymond RR, circa 1924, 21J 16 size, GF, up-down indicator, **$795-$1,295.**

Elgin/Montgomery dial RR, 6 size 21J, GF, incorrect bow, **$225-$495.**

A 1960s' Swiss Elgin movement view.

Elgin, Swiss, circa 1960s, OF, 16 size, 17J base metal, **$75-$175.**

Elgin, Father Time RR, 16 size 21J movement, **$200-$475.**

Elgin, circa 1919, note sub-seconds at 3:00, 15J 16 size, WGF/metal dial, **$65-$175.**

Watch case company
ad inside pocket
watch case.

Elgin PW movement
shipping box,
circa 1922, 12 size,
$10-$20.

Elgin, circa 1904, 14k,
multi-colored HC.

Elgin, circa 1904, 14k multi-colored HC,
light blue fancy dial, 15J, **$695-$995.**

Elgin, 17J 12 size, movement view.

Elgin, flip-out stand, circa 1927, 17J 12 size, white gold, **$494-$795.**

Elgin, 12S, 15J movement.

Elgin, circa 1920, 15J 12 size, GF OF, **$95-$195.**

Elgin, circa 1920s, GF pink OF, 12 size, **$295-$495.**

Elgin, circa 1930s, 7J 16 size, WGF OF, **$125-$200.**

Elgin, Dexter Street movement.

Elgin, Dexter Street.

Elgin, "Dexter Street," circa 1873, 10 size, KW KS, 14k, **$295-$795.**

Elgin, 14k
engraved bird
motif case.

Elgin, circa 1886, 11J 6 size, 14k HC, **$295-$795.**

Elgin movement.

Elgin, circa 1888,
6 size, GF HC LS,
$295-$595.

Elgin case front.

Elgin case back.

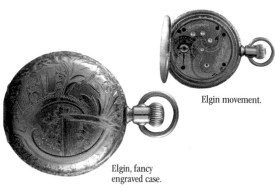

Elgin movement.

Elgin, fancy
engraved case.

Elgin, circa 1895, 7J 0 size,
GF HC, **$95-$295.**

Gruen

Gruen, Veri-Thin Swiss, circa 1910, fancy engraved metal dial, GF, **$200-$350.**

Gruen, Veri-Thin, original papers.

Gruen, Veri Thin, circa 1920, GF, 17J, pentagon
shape, fancy enamel detail, **$195-$495.**

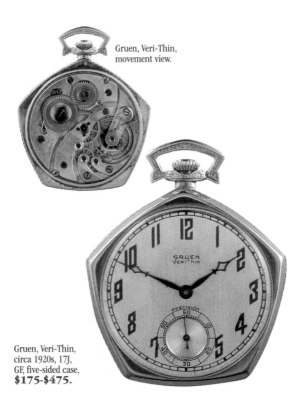

Gruen, Veri-Thin,
movement view.

Gruen, Veri-Thin,
circa 1920s, 17J,
GF, five-sided case,
$175-$475.

Gruen, Veri-Thin, 15J,
movement view.

Gruen, Veri-Thin with
copper dial, circa 1930s,
15J, GF, **$100-$200.**

Hamilton Watch Co., Lancaster, Pennsylvania

Founded in 1892, this company is regarded by many collectors as the overall premier watch manufacturer in American history. The company produced high-quality watches and was popular in the railroad industry. The master watchmaker I worked for in the 1970s timed every watch that left the store up against a Hamilton 992B pocket watch that hung on a nail in the watch repair room. Hamilton made watchmaking history when it introduced its electric battery-powered wrist watch in 1957. Hamilton railroad pocket watches are sought after by collectors, as are examples from the large wrist-watch line it produced.

Hamilton factory scene, celluloid advertising item, 1900s.

Hamilton, 19J movement.

Hamilton, Grade 944, circa 1905, 19J 18 size, five position, display type case, **$275-$575.**

Hamilton, 946 movement view.

Hamilton 946, Parks
Jewelers-Dauphine,
Manitoba, Canada,
circa 1905, 23J 18 size,
$695-$1,195.

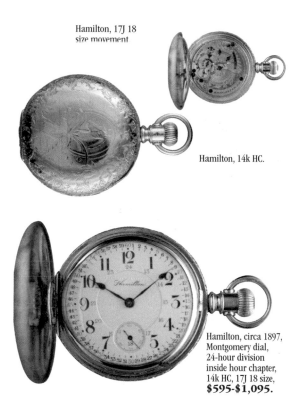

Hamilton, 17J 18
size movement

Hamilton, 14k HC.

Hamilton, circa 1897,
Montgomery dial,
24-hour division
inside hour chapter,
14k HC, 17J 18 size,
$595-$1,095.

Hamilton, 992, RR movement.

Hamilton, 992, circa
1909, 21J 16 size, silver
case, **$295-$595.**

Hamilton, circa 1919, 992 Time King, 21J 16 size, **$295-$595.**

Hamilton, circa 1919, 16 size, 21J, montgomery dial 992, WGF case is marked Hamilton Railroad Model, **$295-$595.**

Hamilton 992L movement.

Hamilton 992L, circa 1932,
very bold dial, 21J 16 size,
GF, **$295-$595.**

Model 950, 23J movement, circa 1932.

Hamilton, model 950, circa 1932, Montgomery dial, 16 size, 23J, 14k GF, **$1,000-$1,500.**

Hamilton, 992 movement.

Hamilton, Model 992L,
circa 1932, 21J 16 size,
WGF, signed Ham.,
case with solid bow,
$395-$895.

Hamilton, 992B movement.

Hamilton RR, 992B, circa 1942, 21J 16 size, YGF, signed Ham. case, **$395-$795.**

Hamilton, 992B Railway
Special, circa 1942,
21J, GF, two-tone case,
$325-$625.

Hamilton,
chronograph/Grade
23, circa WW II, nickel
plate, **$295-$495.**

Hamilton, 4992B
movement, Greenwich
Civil Time.

Hamilton, 4992B,
GCT (Greenwich
Civil Time),
circa 1942, 22J,
chrome case/24-
hour black dial,
$395-$595.

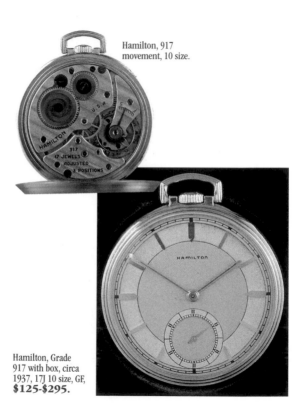

Hamilton, 917 movement, 10 size.

Hamilton, Grade 917 with box, circa 1937, 17J 10 size, GF, **$125-$295.**

Presentation 23J
Movement, adjusted
to five positions,
swing-out case.

Hamilton Presentation Watch with coin holder fob,
circa 1920, 14k, 12 size model 920 23J, **$595-$895.**

Hampden Watch Co., Canton, Ohio

Founded in the late 1870s, this company produced watches, the vast majority being pocket type, up until the early 1930s when it was bought by the Russians, who used the company to start watch manufacturing in that country.

Hampden, John Hancock model, circa 1910, 18 size 21J GF HC Ferguson dial, **$2,000-$2,400.**

Photo courtesy of Antiquorum.

18S lever set
movement.

Hampden Dueber,
circa 1902, 18 size
lever set base metal
case, **$75-$150.**

William McKinley movement.

Hampden, William
McKinley, circa
1917, 16 size 17J
10k GF, metal dial,
$100-$200.

Hampden Chronometer, 21J movement.

Hampden Chronometer, circa 1915, double sunk dial, GF, 21J 16 size, **$295-$400.**

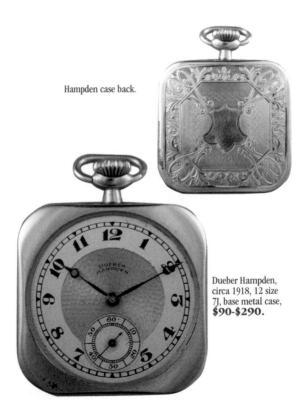

Hampden case back.

Dueber Hampden,
circa 1918, 12 size
7J, base metal case,
$90-$290.

Model 306 movement.

Hampden, Model 306, circa 1912, GF 15J 12 size, double sunk dial, **$100-$200.**

Hampden, 17 J 12 size, "Minute Man" movement.

Hampden, the "Minute Man," circa 1920, 17J 12 size, white gold-filled case two-tone dial, **$90-$290.**

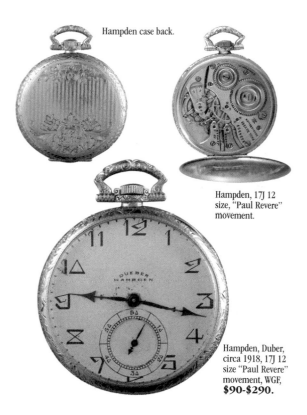

Hampden case back.

Hampden, 17J 12 size, "Paul Revere" movement.

Hampden, Duber, circa 1918, 17J 12 size "Paul Revere" movement, WGF, **$90-$290.**

Hampden movement.

Hampden, circa 1891,
6 size, 14k multicolor
HC, **$500-$1,000.**

Molly Stark movement.

Hampden Molly Stark, circa 1910, 3/0 size 7J, GF hunter case, **$100-$225.**

Hebdomas, Swiss, exposed balance, silver and Niello case, fancy dial, **$395-$595.**

Swiss Hebdomas 8 day, circa 1900s-1920s, silver cased exposed balance pin set, **$200-$400.**

E. Howard & Co., Boston, Massachusetts

Edward Howard, a pioneer in American watch history, produced excellent pocket watches with his company. Complete watches in their original cases are extremely collectible and sought after. The company was sold to the Keystone Watchcase Company in 1903. It continued producing fine quality pocket watches until 1930.

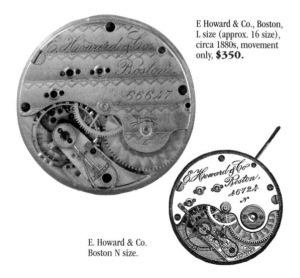

E Howard & Co., Boston, L size (approx. 16 size), circa 1880s, movement only, **$350.**

E. Howard & Co. Boston N size.

E Howard & Co., Boston,
circa 1870s, N size (approx.
18 size), transition period
pendant set, 18k HC,
$1,500-$2,800.

E Howard & Co., Boston,
N size (approx. 18
size) movement.

Howard-Keystone, 16 size 21J movement.

Howard-Keystone, circa 1910, 21J 16 size, nickel display-type case, **$295-$595.**

Howard, Series 11
movement view.

Howard-Keystone,
Series 11, circa
1913, 21J 16 size,
$395-$795.

Howard movement,
circa 1915, 16 size 17J.

Howard, circa 1915
OF, 16 size 17J WGF,
$195-$295.

Illinois Watch Co., Springfield, Illinois

Founded in 1869, this prolific company turned out to be the third largest producer behind Elgin and Waltham in terms of numbers of jeweled watches produced. In 1927, the company was sold to Hamilton. Its fine-quality pocket watches were popular among railroadmen, and the line of wrist watches it produced is highly collectible.

Illinois, Bunn Special, circa 1903, 24J 18 size, movement view, **$1,000-$1,500.**

Illinois, circa 1880, 18 size, silver,
very rare floral dial, **$595-$995.**

Movement view Iowa Watch Co., key wind.

Iowa Watch Co., Illinois model 1, circa 1880s, nickel, 18 size 11J, lever set, **$195-$395.**

Illinois, 18 size movement view.

Illinois, circa 1896, 18 size, display case, 17J two-tone checkerboard movement, Chalmer pat. Regulator, **$195-$395.**

Two-tone Illinois movement view, The Accurate Time.

Illinois, "The Accurate Time," circa 1898, dial marked Sloan & Feinberg, 18 size, base metal, double sunk dial, **$195-$395.**

Illinois, Bunn Special, circa 1904, 24J 18 size, silver swing-out case, **$1,000-$1,500.**

Illinois, case back train scene.

Illinois movement, swing-out case. This is the movement of the Illinois Bun Special watch.

Washington Watch Co., Illinois movement.

Washington Watch Co., Illinois "Liberty Bell," circa 1906, 17J 18 size, OF nickel case, **$100-$300.**

Illinois, 11J KW movement, locomotive on movement.

Illinois, "Locomotive," circa 1887, 11J 18 size KW transition, 4 oz OF silver case, **$295-$595.**

23J two-tone movement.

Illinois Sagamo, circa 1902, 23J 16 size, two-tone movement, **$795-$1,295.**

Movement view
Burlington Watch Co.

Illinois, Burlington
Watch Co.,
circa 1919, OF,
16 Size GF 21J,
montgomery dial,
$195-$395.

Illinois, Bunn
Special movement.

Illinois, Bunn Special,
circa 1923, 23J 16 size,
nickel swing-out case,
$695-$1,495.

Sagamo Special, movement view.

Illinois, Sagamo
Special, circa 1925,
23J, solid bow,
$895-$1,395.

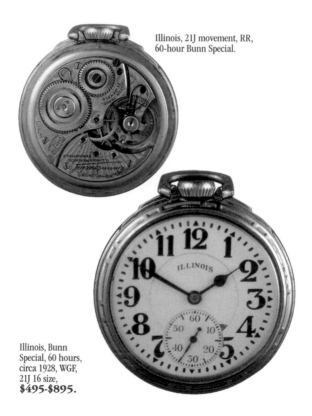

Illinois, 21J movement, RR, 60-hour Bunn Special.

Illinois, Bunn Special, 60 hours, circa 1928, WGF, 21J 16 size, **$495-$895.**

Inside case back.

Illinois, Bunn Special, Grade 161A, circa 1938, 21J 16 size GF, movement view, **$1,000-$2,000.**

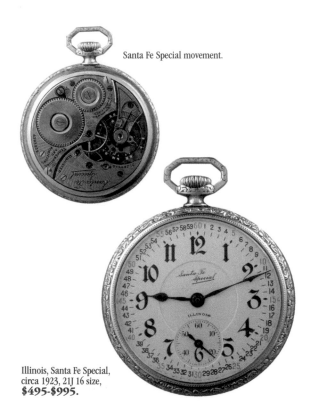

Santa Fe Special movement.

Illinois, Santa Fe Special,
circa 1923, 21J 16 size,
$495-$995.

Illinois, fancy GF hunter case, rare fancy
dial with butterfly, 16 size, **$595-$995.**

Illinois, circa 1910, 17
J, three-finger bridge,
$100-$225.

Illinois, Burlington Special, three-finger bridge movement.

Illinois, Burlington Special 16 size, circa 1910, 19J adj., GF, **$150-$350.**

Illinois movement, Sears
and Roebuck Special.

Illinois, Sears
and Roebuck
Special, circa
1902, 17J 16 size,
$125-$250.

Illinois Autocrat
movement view.

Illinois Autocrat,
circa 1924, GF, 17J 12
size, **$195-$395.**

Ingersoll (Robert H. Ingersoll & Bro.), New York, New York

Founded in 1881, it produced inexpensive, non-jeweled, "dollar" watches. When competition became fierce among watch companies, Ingersoll sold its watches for $1.

Ingersoll movement ad.

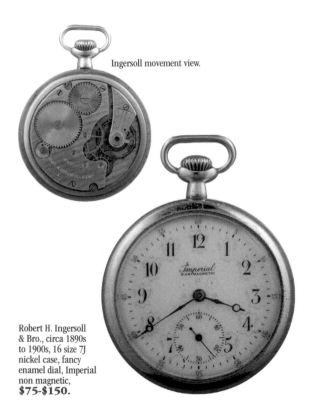

Ingersoll movement view.

Robert H. Ingersoll
& Bro., circa 1890s
to 1900s, 16 size 7J
nickel case, fancy
enamel dial, Imperial
non magnetic,
$75-$150.

Ingersoll, Reliance, 16 size 7J movement.

Ingersoll, Reliance, circa 1894, 16 size 7J, nickel, **$50-$100.**

Ingraham (E. Ingraham Company), Bristol, Connecticut

E. Ingraham Co., Sentinel rotating digital seconds, walnut wood case, used in chess matches, **$75-$150 each.**

E. Ingraham, master, approx.18 size
dollar watch, metal dial, **$40-$75.**

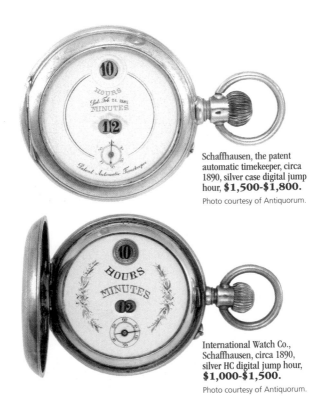

Schaffhausen, the patent automatic timekeeper, circa 1890, silver case digital jump hour, **$1,500-$1,800.**

Photo courtesy of Antiquorum.

International Watch Co., Schaffhausen, circa 1890, silver HC digital jump hour, **$1,000-$1,500.**

Photo courtesy of Antiquorum.

Le Coultre pocket alarm in box.

Le Coultre-Swiss, circa 1940s, pocket alarm, brushed aluminum, **$400-$700.**

Lemania movement, Swiss.

Lemania-Swiss,
chronograph, circa
1930s, black military
dial, chrome case,
$495-$895.

Longines, Switzerland

Longines movement.

Longines, circa 1878, IIJ, nickel, **$95-$295.**

Longines case
front with fob.

Longines-Swiss, circa 1885, HC LS, 800 silver, **$250-$450.**

Longines
movement
view.

Longines, J.B. Hudson
& Son, circa 1920s,
14k 17J 5 adjustments,
$295-$495.

The first Longines watch, caliber 840 hand-winding mechanical movement, circa 1867, HC silver pocket watch, white dial inscribed with 12 Roman numerals, sub-seconds at 6 o' clock.

Photo courtesy Longines Museum Collection.

Circa 1920 19-ligne minute repeater movement, chronograph, enameled 18kt HC with gold dial, Breguet-style numerals.

Photo courtesy Longines Museum Collection.

Circa 1919 HC set with diamonds, rubies and emeralds, personalized with a monogram, dial enhanced with painted Arabic numerals.

Photo courtesy Longines Museum Collection.

Movado, Swizerland

In 1881, Achille Ditesheim, barely 19 years old and fresh out of watchmaking school, founded his own watchmaking company and was soon joined by three of his brothers. In 1905, a new modern factory was built and a new company name was introduced: Movado. Movado means "always in motion" in the international language of Esperanto—a language based on words with roots commonly found in the romance languages. Esperanto was very popular among cosmopolitan circles throughout Europe, providing an interesting insight into the Ditesheim's vision for its company.

In the first decade of the 20th century, when the market was still geared to pocket watches, Movado advanced the development of the wrist-watch movement. The company was regarded as a pioneer in miniaturized movements and in 1912 introduced the Polyplan watch. An ultimate in conception, design, and engineering, Polyplan housed one of the earliest patented "form" movements, constructed on three planes inside a curved case that followed the natural contours of the wrist. In 1926, the company launched a new watch design called the Ermeto. One of the most unusual watches ever created, this unique pillow-shaped pocket watch housed a patented movement that was wound by the sliding motion of the case as it was opened and closed. The sections of the two-part metal case opened like curtains to reveal the dial. A single opening provided sufficient winding of the mainspring for four hours running time; with six openings, it would run all day and night. The name "Ermeto" was derived from the Greek word meaning "sealed."

Although not actually air or water tight, the term suggested protection against shock, dust, and temperature changes. Carried

View of the Movado factory in La Chaux-de-Fonds, circa 1955.
Photo courtesy of Movado Watch Co.

loose or attached to a chain, Ermeto was known as the only watch suitable for both men and women—a novel concept at the time. The 1930s were productive years for Movado. The factory developed its two-button Chronograph wrist watches with calendar indications that even included moon phases. Movado began production of wrist watches with automatic winding in 1945, and in 1946 it introduced the Calendomatic. These self-winding wrist watches of the 1940s are still among the most nostalgic collectibles ever produced by Movado. The next technological advancement in automatic watches came in 1956 with the introduction of the Kingmatic, a series of rotor-driven timepieces.

A prophetic moment for Movado occurred in 1947 when Nathan George Horwitt, an adherent of the Bauhaus design movement and one of America's outstanding designers, set out to simplify the wrist watch. His solution was to become a legend in modern design known as the Movado Museum Watch. "We do not know time as a number sequence," he said, "but by the position of the sun as the earth rotates." Applying this theory, he eliminated the numerals from the dial. Strongly influenced by the clean, spare lines of the Bauhaus, he designed a dial defined by a single gold dot symbolizing the sun at high noon, the hands suggesting the movement of the earth.

Horwitt's prototype was selected by the Museum of Modern Arts in 1959 for its permanent collection. The name, the Museum Watch, is so integral to the company's image that to many it is the first timepiece that comes to mind when they think of Movado.

Movado, chronometer, circa 1920s, 18k gold, rare shaped case, **$2,400-$3,000.**

Movado inside case back, stamp with hand-holding pocket watch.

Movado, circa 1930, Swiss steel case.

Movado, circa 1930s, metal dial, gold applied numbers, **$150-$400.**

Two Movado deck watches in original test cases.

Photo courtesy of Movado Watch Co.

Movado, minute repeating calendar chronograph, circa 1905, 18k hunter case.

Photo courtesy of Movado Watch Co.

Movado, circa 1935, watch set in brown leather-bound book titled Livre d' Heures, caliber 150 MN movement.

Photo courtesy Movado.

Ulysse Nardin, Switzerland

Founded in 1846, this renowned company is known for its early high-precision marine chronometers. In 1935, Ulysse Nardin developed the caliber 22-24, the first Chronometer with split second fly-back hands measuring 1/10th of a second. Used at the Berlin Olympic Games in 1936, they earned the company many Gold medals and Grand Prix prizes for their accuracy and perfection. This company still produces extremely high-quality complicated watches to this day.

Ulysse Nardin, HC chronograph, circa late 1800s, **$2,000-$2,500.**

Photo courtesy Ulysse Nardin.

Ulysse Nardin, engraved case inscribed "US Corp of Engineers, USA No. 9267."

Ulysse Nardin-Swiss, circa 1910s, enamel dial radium numbers, silver, **$450-$750.**

Ulysse Nardin, split-second chronograph, circa 1890, silver 23J, **$2,500-$3,000.**

Photo courtesy of Antiquorum.

Pocket chronometer-chronograph, made for the Chicago Exhibition of 1893, 18k and silver.

Photo courtesy of Ulysse Nardin.

Ulysse Nardin, circa 1912, Deck Chronometer, sterling, **$1,500-$2,000.**

Photo courtesy of Antiquorum.

Ulysse Nardin, circa 1940, deck chronometer with power reserve indicator, **$3,000-$4,000.**

Photo courtesy of Antiquorum.

New Haven (New Haven Clock Co.)
New Haven, Conn., 1853-1946

New Haven, examples of the Tip-Top, **$25-$75.**

New Haven movement view.

New Haven, pin lever, chrome case dollar watch, **$65-$95.**

16 size movement view.

Non-Magnetic Watch Co., Swiss made for American market, circa 1890s, 16 size, nickel, **$150-$300.**

New York Standard Watch Co., Jersey City, NJ

New York Standard
movement view, 7J.

New York Standard, circa
1900s, 0 size 7J GP, enamel
dial, pocket or pendant/early
wrist watch, **$75-$150.**

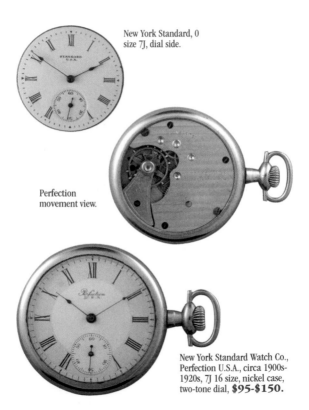

New York Standard, 0 size 7J, dial side.

Perfection movement view.

New York Standard Watch Co., Perfection U.S.A., circa 1900s-1920s, 7J 16 size, nickel case, two-tone dial, **$95-$150.**

Omega, Switzerland

Omega case back.

Photo courtesy of Antiquorum.

Omega, circa 1905,
14k multicolored HC
fancy dial, 16 size, 21J,
$4,000-$5,000.

Photo courtesy of Antiquorum.

Omega, Philippine Expedition, circa 1899, caliber 19, enamel artwork.
Photo courtesy of Omega.

Omega, circa 1930s, 15J,
unusual stainless case,
$250-$450.

Omega, 14k OF, rare
dial, **$495-$895.**

Omega, movement view.

Omega-Swiss, circa 1974, stainless steel, hacking feature, **$195-$395.**

Patek Philippe, Switzerland

Founded in 1839 and considered to be one of the most important watchmakers in the world, this high-end company produced, and still creates, incredible works of the watchmaking art. These watches are built to last and have been purchased throughout its 160-plus-year history by notables the likes of Queen Victoria, Kipling, Einstein, Tolstoy, and Marie Curie. Every Patek is collectible.

Patek Philippe, Shreve & Co., San Francisco, circa 1882, chronograph 18k HC Photoon dial, 21J, **$5,000-$6,000.**

Photo courtesy of Antiquorum.

Patek Philippe, Switzerland, movement view.

Patek Philippe, A.H. Rodanet & Co. Paris, circa 1870s, 18k, Roman numerals, **$2,000-$3,000.**

Patek Philippe & Cie, presentation watch, circa 1920s, 18k, 18J, **$2,000-$3,000.**

Patek Philippe, Bailey Banks & Biddle, minute repeater with split-second chronograph, circa 1913, 18k 40J 8 adjustments, **$18,000-$22,000.**

Photo courtesy of Antiquorum.

Patek Philippe, Switzerland,
movement view.

Patek Philippe, Shreve
& Co., circa 1896,
18k pink gold case,
unusual sweep second,
$2,500-$3,500.

Patek Philippe, movement view.

Patek Philippe, R. J. Richards
Co., Massachusetts, circa
1920s, 18k, 18J 8 adj.,
$2,000-$3,000.

Patek case, dust cover view.

Patek movement.

Patek Philippe, ladies
pendant monogrammed
case, circa 1900,
12 Ligne 18k HC,
$1,800-$2,500.

Rockford Watch Co.
Rockford, Illinois, 1874-1915

Early Rockford movement view.

Rockford Watch Co., circa 1870s, silver HC,
18 size, key wind key set, **$295-$495.**

Rockford Watch Co., circa
1880s, rare 24-hour dial,
18 size KW transition,
$1,200-$1,700.

Rockford Watch Co.,
circa 1886, 15J 18 size,
GF fancy engraved
HC, **$195-$395.**

Rockford Watch Co., circa 1882, 18 size 11J lever set, sub seconds at 3 o'clock, 14k, **$1,200-$1,700.**

Photo courtesy of Antiquorum.

Rockford Watch Co., circa 1899, 18 size 16J GF, fancy dial, **$1,200-$1,500.**

Photo courtesy of Antiquorum.

Rockford rare aluminum movement.

Photo courtesy of Antiquorum.

Rockford Watch Co., circa 1900, 16 size 15J very rare aluminum movement, in nickel display case, est., **$6,500-$8,500.**

Photo courtesy of Antiquorum.

Rockford Watch Co., circa 1904, unusual
red dial, 16 size 15J, **$2,000-$2,500.**

Photo courtesy of Antiquorum.

Rockford watch ad.

Early Seiko movement.

Seiko, Seikosha
Precision, circa 1930s,
16 size, chrome case,
$250-$500.

South Bend Watch Co. South Bend, Indiana, 1903-1929

South Bend, Grade 227, 21J 16 size RR.

South Bend, Grade 227 RR, circa 1928, 21J 16 size, double sunk dial, **$250-$500.**

South Bend Watch Co.,
OF Montgomery dial RR,
$250-$500.

South Bend Watch Co.,
circa 1928, model 429, OF
12 size, **$100-$200.**

South Bend Watch Co.

South Bend Watch Co.,
Studebaker, circa 1927, 21J
12 size, GF, **$200-$400.**

Trenton Watch Co., 7J movement.

Trenton Watch Co., engraved case.

Trenton Watch Co., circa 1891, HC LS, 7J 18 size, GF, **$95-$295.**

Vacheron Constantin-Switzerland

One of the oldest Swiss watch companies, tracing back to the 1700s, it has created some of the most beautiful watches the world has ever seen. Vacheron Constantin ranks among the top makers and is still in existence today. Its high-quality timepieces are extremely collectible and valuable.

Vacheron & Constantin, circa 1955, deck chronometer, power reserve indicator, silver, **$3,500-$4,500.**

Photo courtesy of Antiquorum.

Vacheron Constantin, with a fancy engraved case.

Vacheron Constantin-Swiss, circa 1870s, 18k fancy engraved HC, **$1,750-$2,500.**

Vacheron Constantin-Swiss, presentation watch, inscribed case.

Vacheron Constantin-Swiss, presentation watch circa 1949, rare aluminum case, **$1,500-$2,500.**

Waltham Watch Co.
(American Waltham Watch Co.)
Waltham, Massachusetts

This is the granddaddy of large American watch companies. Its beginnings are in the early 1850s and it produced high-quality watches of every grade. Early examples of Waltham timepieces are valuable collectors' items, and highly sought after. This company was always very innovative, and the pioneering spirit of the people who worked at Waltham led to the development of the machinery that built the watch industry in this country.

Waltham, 6 oz. case back.

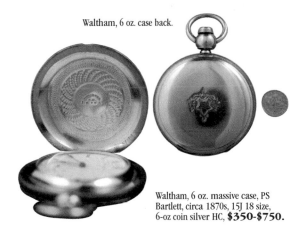

Waltham, 6 oz. massive case, PS Bartlett, circa 1870s, 15J 18 size, 6-oz coin silver HC, **$350-$750.**

Waltham, Elk motif on case.

Waltham, circa 1884,
14k Elk motif box
hinge HC, 11J 18 size,
$850-$1,650.

Crescent St. movement view.

Waltham, Crescent St., circa 1888, model 1883, 18 size 15J, nickel swing-out case, **$195-$295.**

Waltham, Model 1883, circa
1888, GF OF 18 size, fancy dial-
bird scene, **$400-$700.**

American Waltham, circa
1890s, 18 size, nickel case,
fancy dial, **$250-$550.**

Waltham, RR 17J, Canadian Pacific Railway, beaver logo, movement view.

Waltham, Model 1883, Canadian Pacific Railway, circa 1888, 17J 18 size, **$500-$1,000.**

Waltham, Model 1883, Appleton Tracy movement view.

Waltham, Model 1883, circa 1887, 18 size Appleton Tracy movement, nickel display case, **$125-$250.**

845 21J
movement view.

845 21J RR case back.

Waltham, circa 1904,
18 size, 1J grade,
845 RR, base metal,
$295-$495.

Santa Fe Route,
movement view.

Waltham "Santa
Fe Route," circa
1892, 17J 18 size,
$595-$1,195.

Waltham, circa 1903, Vanguard movement view, 19J 18 size, **$175-$400.**

Waltham, unusual case back with engraving, balance exposed to show a bicycle wheel.

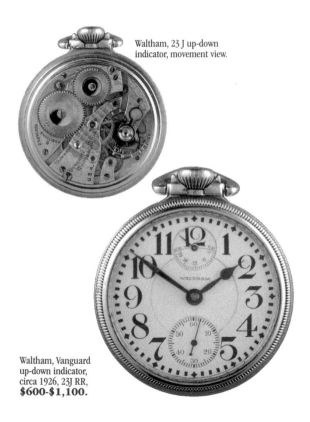

Waltham, 23 J up-down indicator, movement view.

Waltham, Vanguard up-down indicator, circa 1926, 23J RR, **$600-$1,100.**

Waltham Vanguard, movement view.

Waltham, Premier Vanguard, circa 1942, 23J 16 size, RR, GF, **$200-$350.**

Waltham Riverside movement.

Waltham, Riverside Maximus, circa 1901, 23J 16 size PS, **$495-$995.**

Waltham Vanguard, 16 size 19J, movement view.

Waltham Vanguard, circa 1902, 19J 16 size, double sunk dial, **$150-$350.**

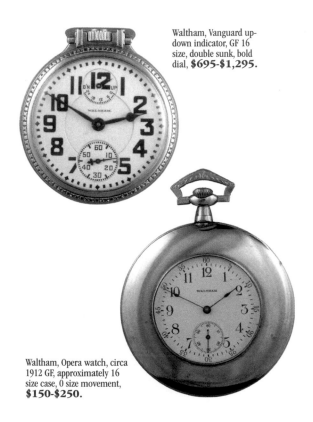

Waltham, Vanguard up-down indicator, GF 16 size, double sunk, bold dial, **$695-$1,295.**

Waltham, Opera watch, circa 1912 GF, approximately 16 size case, 0 size movement, **$150-$250.**

17J movement view.

Waltham, circa 1913,
16 size 17J lever set,
nickel swing-out case,
$150-$225.

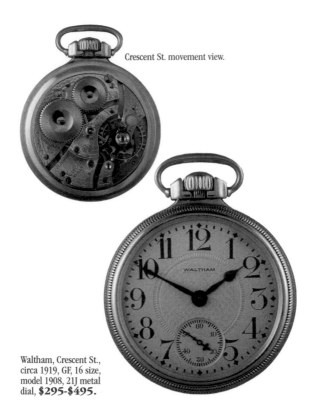

Crescent St. movement view.

Waltham, Crescent St.,
circa 1919, GF, 16 size,
model 1908, 21J metal
dial, **$295-$495.**

Waltham, Equity, circa 1920, 16 size GF 15J, **$100-$150.**

Waltham, fancy dial, GF OF, 16 size, **$250-$350.**

Waltham, circa 1885, 14 size, GF HC, fancy pink and green floral dial, **$250-$700.**

Waltham, circa 1885, LS, 6 size, 11J OF, 14k, **$150-$275.**

Waltham fancy case.

Waltham, circa 1905, 14k
HC, gold and enamel dial,
7J O size, **$495-$795.**

Waltham, circa 1920, 17J 12 size, WGF case, metal dial, **$125-$225.**

Waltham, circa 1923, 17J 12 size, 14k white/personalized dial, **$195-$395.**

Waltham, circa 1891, 15J GF, fancy dial with blue inner chapters and red dots, 6 size HC, **$195-$395.**

American Waltham, circa 189 4, OF, GF, 6 size, fancy dial, **$150-$225.**

Waltham, circa 1887,
6 size LS 7J, 14k,
$150-$295.

Waltham case front view.

Waltham case back.

Waltham movement view.

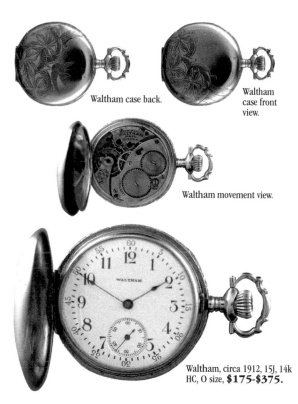

Waltham case back.

Waltham case front view.

Waltham movement view.

Waltham, circa 1912, 15J, 14k HC, O size, **$175-$375.**

Case back view.

Waltham, circa 1891,
OF, 14k, 0 size, fancy
dial, **$795-$995.**

Multi-colored case.

Waltham, circa 1900,
0 size hunter, 14k
with peacock on case,
$895-$1,195.

Waltham, enamel portrait hand-painted on case.

Waltham, 2/0 size, high grade movement.

Waltham, 14k fancy case.

Waltham, 2/0 size, circa 1889, set with 76 diamonds on front and rear, enamel portrait hand painted on case back, high grade movement, **$3,500-$5,000.**

Waterbury Watch Co., Waterbury, Conn.

Waterbury Watch Co.,
Addison movement.

Waterbury Watch Co.,
Addison Series N, circa
1890s, duplex escapement,
silver case, **$75-$95.**

Waterbury Watch Co., Addison, GF series N, 0 size, fancy dial and hands, **$95-$195.**

Waterbury Watch Co., 0 size, Duplex movement, silver case, blue blister-type enamel dial, **$95-$195.**

Case back view, 1895 engraving.

Series K movement.

Waterbury Watch Co.,
Addison, series K, Duplex
escapement, 18 size,
GF, **$95-$195.**

Wyler-Swiss, The Skipper, circa 1950s, 17J incaflex, chrome case, **$75-$150.**

Zenith Swiss, unusual alarm pocket watch, PS circa 1910s, nickel case-enamel dial, missing hand, **$300-$450.**

Miscellaneous Swiss Watches

Movement view, key
wind key set.

Swiss made for English, H.
Samuel Manchester, "Acme
Lever," 17 ligne silver KW
KS, **$200-$350.**

S. Smith & Son 9 Strand,
Watchmakers to the
Admiralty London, Swiss
non magnetizable,
$150-$300.

Aeby, Bellenot & Co., circa
1885, silver gilt HC, jumphour,
$1,500-$1,800.

Photo courtesy of Antiquorum.

Bulova, circa 1920s, GF engraved cdge and bail, 17J fancy metal dial, **$195-$395.**

Swiss, late 1800s, 10J pin-set cylinder, silver case with fancy dial, **$95-$195.**

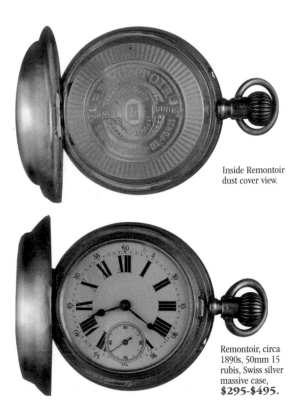

Inside Remontoir dust cover view.

Remontoir, circa 1890s, 50mm 15 rubis, Swiss silver massive case, **$295-$495.**

Swiss watch/timer back view.

Swiss watch and
timer, start-stop sweep
second, silver oversize,
$195-$295.

Swiss Besancon, La Reine des Montres, cylinder movement, GF 24-hour inner chapter, **$95-$195.**

Cartier, circa 1915, platinum, diamonds, rock crystal, **$10,000-$12,000.**

Photo courtesy of Antiquorum.

Audemars Freves, Brassus & Geneve, 45mm 14k hunter case, **$695-$895.**

J. W. Allen, 37 Strand London, circa 1875, oversize Swiss movement, PS, **$250-$450.**

Swiss silver case back.

Swiss silver, fancy dial
flower in center, 18
ligne pin set, Roman
numerals, **$95-$195.**

Swiss Frenia, hand-painted blister-type metal dial pin, lever pin set, GP case, **$75-$175.**

Swiss Pearlham, cylinder movement, enamel blister type dial, base metal case, **$95-$150.**

Back view of Faro engraved case.

Fancy engraved movement.

Swiss Faro, silver cased pin set, blister metal dial, **$95-$195.**

Engraved scene on back with Swiss cross.

Swiss Pin Set, flowers in center of enamel dial, nickel cased, **$150-$250.**

Back view Philippine crest.

Swiss Precaution, gun metal with enamel work on back, pin lever pin set, **$100-$200.**

Swiss Systeme Roskopf, pin lever pin set, 19 ligne base metal case, very fancy flower dial, **$100-$200.**

Swiss, 18 ligne, white and cobalt blue blister dial, gun metal, fancy gold hands, **$95-$150.**

Back view Roskopf.

Swiss Roskopf,
gun metal, pin
lever pin set,
$75-$150.

Case back view.

Swiss Roskopf, Cuervo
y sobrinos Habana,
nickel pin set,
$95-$195.

Movement view,
Greenwood & Bros.

CF Greenwood & Bros.,
Norfolk, VA, very high
grade Swiss movement,
wolf tooth winding, 11.5
ligne 18k, **$295-$495.**

Silver and gold case back.

Swiss silver and gold, heart-shaped cut out dial with flowers, pin set 10J cylinder movement, note: missing hands, **$125-$225.**

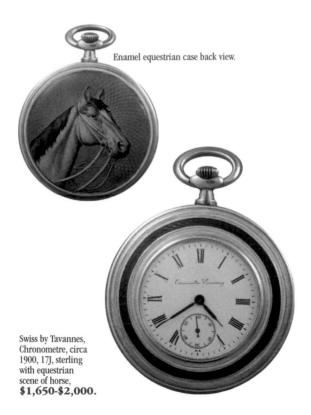

Enamel equestrian case back view.

Swiss by Tavannes,
Chronometre, circa
1900, 17J, sterling
with equestrian
scene of horse,
$1,650-$2,000.

Gold Bridges movement.

Photo courtesy of Antiquorum.

Girard Perregaux, the Golden Bridge, circa 1890, minute repeater with split-second chronograph, 18k 32J, **$10,000-$12,000.**

Photo courtesy of Antiquorum.

Swiss Depose, HC nickel pin set, Brail, blind man's watch, raised brail bumps at hours, heavy duty screwed-on hands, **$150-$250.**

Shreve & Co., circa 1920s, Longines movement, 14k, **$595-$895.**

Movado Ermeto ad, circa 1930s.

Movado Ermeto Chronometer, opening and closing winds movement, black enamel-purse watch, **$295-$495.**

Ermeto with diamonds, blue enamel, circa 1930.

Photo courtesy of Movado Watch Co.

Ermeto purse watch closed.

Movado Ermeto, circa 1940s, purse watch, small size-leather, **$195-$395.**

Movado Ermeto Chronometer, circa 1930s, sterling silver gold wash, winds as you open and close the case, **$295-$495.**

Movado Ermeto purse watch open.

Eterna Swiss, circa 1920s,
silver niello, **$350-$550.**

Rolex, purse watch Sporting
Princess Chronometre, circa
1936, **$3,500-$4,500.**

Photo courtesy of Antiquorum.

Case-open position.

Swiss purse watch, enamel
on silver case with pink roses,
Art Deco, **$195-$395.**

Tissot Swiss Art Deco purse watch, blue-black enamel, **$193-$395.**

Photo courtesy of Tissot.

Swiss Stratford, Langendorf movement, circa 1920s, 6J, GF, **$75-$175.**

Swiss, eight-day movement.

Swiss, circa 1910s, eight-day, visible balance, nickel silver, **$150-$250.**

Unusual enamel and gold dial, gun metal case, **$95-$195.**

Touchon & Co., circa 1925, 17J Swiss, platinum and enamel set with diamonds and rubies, **$4,000-$5,000.**

Photo courtesy of Antiquorum.

Duplex heavily engraved movement.

Unusual Swiss, exposed movement, circa 1930s, **$300-$400.**

Minute Repeater dust cover.

Minute Repeater movement.

Swiss Minute Repeater, circa 1890s, 18k gold HC, **$3,500-$5,500.**

Back view of high relief repoussé case.

Swiss Volta, 1/4 hour repeater, push piece to activate, silver cased, **$1,500-$2,000.**

Swiss HC back.

Swiss, 14k gold HC,
$700-$1,200.

Kienzle Selecta, made in
Germany, 17J shockproof
chrome case, **$150-$250.**

Tiffany & Co., circa 1890,
minute repeater with split-
second chronograph, 18k 32J,
$10,000-$12,000.

Photo courtesy of Antiquorum.

Repeater movement view.

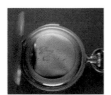

Tiffany engraved dust cover.

Tiffany & Co. front cover view.

Tiffany & Co., five-minute repeater, circa 1900, 18k, **$6,000-$7,000.**

Examples of Niello Pocket Watches Circa 1900s-1920s

Niello is a form of black enamel decoration used mostly on silver watch cases. The designs are deeply engraved into the metal, then filled with the enamel mixture and heated. The silver, or gold inlay high spots, pick out the design. Niello-type cases were used by many fine watch companies such as Rolex, Eterna, and Omega. Depending on the condition, as niello is semi-hard and fragile, and whether it is a well-known watch brand, **values are $250-$1,200 and up.**

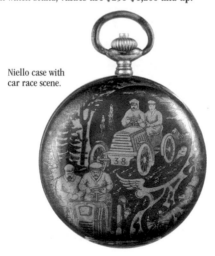

Niello case with car race scene.

Flowers with plate for engraving monogram.

Oriental design.

Demi -hunter back.

Demi-hunter front.

Eterna checkerboard
case back.

Eterna.

Bird on branch.

Hunting scene on horseback.

Case back-Leopard.

Hunter case
front-Lion.

Oriental beauty, gold head ornament.

Floral design.

Art Deco design.

Floral design.

Sunburst design.

Fancy two-tone case
with emblem.

Flowers with plate for engraving monogram.

Fancy scroll design.

Jungle scene.

Woman with hair ornament,
crackle background.

Examples of Repoussé Watches

Repoussé is a style of metalwork where the metal is hammered up from the reverse side to form a design. Depending on the subject portrayed, condition, and size of the case, these artful watches vary in price from **$200 to $500 and up.**

French, circa early 1900s, sterling-dragon scene.

Unusual shape case, back.

Unusual shaped case, floral design.

Art Deco, woman, bird,
and four-leaf clover.

Ducks and dogs.

Case back, pointer.

Three dogs on case.

Case back, poppies.

Silver repoussé case, poppy design.

Omega, 1922 Art Deco, case is 18k gold with floral-enamel
design, cathedral hands with engraved bow gilt dial.

Photo courtesy of Omega.

Omega, circa 1925 Art Deco, 18k, enamel cloisonné case.
Photo courtesy of Omega.

Patek Philippe pendant watch, circa 1890s, blue
enamel and diamond, **$3,000-$5,000.**

Swiss ladies pendant watch, enamel and gold case, **$150-$300.**

Wrist Watches

Audemars Piguet, circa 1968, 18k, **$3,500-$4,500.**

Photo courtesy of Antiquorum.

Benrus, circa 1940s, GF case, sub-seconds/large lugs, **$95-$195.**

Benrus, circa 1920s-30s, square two tone, chrome with gold bezel, 15J, **$95-$195.**

Alpha, circa late 1940s early 1950s, 18k pink, black dial, large teardrop lugs, **$500-$700.**

Baume & Mercier, flip-top watch open.

Baum & Mercier, bracelet with fliptop, circa 1950s, 14k, diamonds, .75ct. total wt., **$995-$1,495.**

Benrus, circa late 1930s early 1940s, GF stainless back, 17J, **$75-$125.**

Benrus, circa late 1940s, day date, GF stainless back, 17J, **$95-$195.**

Benrus, rotating bezel, manual wind, stainless, **$75-$150.**

Benrus, circa 1950s, 21J GF, fancy lugs, **$100-$200.**

Blancpain, Switzerland

Since 1735, Blancpain, the world's oldest watch brand, has symbolized the finest in traditional mechanical watch making. Through its famous slogan, "Since 1735, there has never been a quartz Blancpain watch, and there never will be," the brand has consistently made clear its determination to perpetuate this remarkable know-how, the pride of Swiss watch making.

In 1926, Blancpain contributed to watch history by producing the prototype of the first wrist watch with an "automatic"-wind mechanism, for the famous "Harwood," the invention of John Harwood an English horologist. In 1953, Blancpain released the "Fifty Fathoms." As one of the first diver watches to be water-resistant to 50 fathoms (300 feet), it would soon become a precious working tool for divers the world over. Jacques Coustcau and his divers wore this watch when they made the film, "The World of Silence," in 1956, and it was soon recognized and adopted by the armed forces of several nations, like the U.S. Navy and the French and German armies. This famous firm still produces mechanical watches to this day and is regarded as one of the top makers.

Blancpain, Fifty Fathoms divers' watches, stainless
steel-automatic, circa 1950s, **$1,500-$3,000.**

Bovet-Swiss, chronograph, two register, circa 1940s, stainless case with square pushers, **$495-$895.**

Ernest Borel, circa 1950s, 18k square case, **$250-$500.**

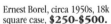

Ernest Borel, cocktail, circa 1960s, automatic, stainless, **$95-$195.**

Breitling Chronograph, circa 1940s, triple date, 18k pink, **$1,000-$2,000.**

Photo courtesy of Antiquorum.

Breitling, Datora chronograph, circa 1952, SS triple date, **$1,600-$2,000.**

Photo courtesy of Antiquorum.

Breitling Geneve Navitimer, chronograph, circa 1960s, black dial, white bezel, **$1,200-$1,600.**

Breitling, Navitimer
model 806, circa 1967,
three register, stainless,
$1,000 to $1,800.

Breitling, Chronomat,
chronograph automatic,
circa 1970s, SS,
$700-$900.

Photo courtesy of
Antiquorium.

Breitling, Navitimer
Chrono-matic, circa
1970s, SS black dial,
$800-$1,000.

Photo courtesy of
Antiquorium.

Breitling, chronograph
three register, stainless,
$900-$1,100.

Breitling, Navitimer, rare date model timer lower
right corner, stainless, **$1,500-$2,500.**

Bulova

This highly successful American watch company is noted for its Art Deco wrist watches of the 1920s and 1930s, and for the huge success of its "Accutron" tuning-fork watch, produced well into the 1970s.

Bulova case back.

Bulova, ladies, circa 1920s, unusual 19k engraved case, engraved sterling silver dial, **$100-$250.**

Group of seven Bulova ladies watches, circa 1920s, 1930s and 1940s, GF, **$45-$95 each.**

Blue enamel and 14k
bow design, back.

Bulova ladies, rare blue enamel
and 14k bow design, ribbon
band, **$495-$795.**

Bulova, circa 1920s, chrome stepped case, radium hands with sub-seconds, **$75-$175.**

Bulova, circa 1940s, diamonds, 23J, 14k WG, **$195-$395.**

Bulova, circa 1940s, 14k, square, 17J, **$175-$350.**

Bulova, circa 1940s, 17J, diamond dial, GF, **$125-$225.**

Bulova, identical pair, pink GF, circa 1930s
to 1940s, 15J, **$95-$195 each.**

Bulova, "Senator," circa 1940s, sub seconds, GF, original box, **$200-$450.**

A small Bulova watch movement.

Bulova, circa 1930s, chrome tank case engraved bezel, sub-seconds, **$95-$195.**

Bulova, back dated 1939.

Bulova, circa 1939, gold filled, unusual case, two tone black and gray dial, **$200-$400.**

Bulova, circa 1966, GF, 30J, self winding, unusual date window at 4:00, **$100-$250.**

Bulova, Accutron 214, circa 1966 (M6), GF, **$175-$275.**

Bulova, circa 1950, 17J Duo Wind, GF, stainless back, **$95-$195.**

Bulova, circa 1955, self winding, GF stainless back, fancy large lugs, **$95-$195.**

Bulova, circa 1955,
21J, ribbed bezel,
$95-$195.

Bulova, circa 1955, GF,
17J, fancy bezel, sub
seconds, **$95-$195.**

Bulova, circa 1959, 17J, self winding, GF with black dial, **$95-$195.**

Bulova, asymmetrical case, circa 1960, 23J GP, stainless back, **$495-$695.**

Bulova, circa 1963, 17J,
stainless, black dial,
$75-$125.

Bulova, circa 1965, 17J
GF, stainless back, sub
seconds, **$75-$125.**

Bulova, circa 1950s, WGF case, hidden lugs, **$75-$175.**

Restored Bulova, circa 1950s, gold filled diamond dial, after dial restoration, **$95-$195.**

Bulova, Accutron 214, circa 1967 (M7), stainless/unusual lugs, **$200-$400.**

Bulova, circa 1966, 10k gold plate, stainless back, 17J, sub seconds, fancy case, **$95-$195.**

Bulova, "Sea King," circa 1969 date, stainless, **$75-$125.**

Bulova Spaceview, Accutron model 214, circa 1971, see through crystal case, stainless, **$250-$395.**

Bulova, digital LED, 1970s, gold tone, **$150-$300.**

Bulova, automatic/ day date, circa 1972, stainless, 23J, **$95-$195.**

Bulova, automatic date, circa 1973, GP, **$95-$195.**

Bulova, Accutron model 218, circa 1973, stainless, **$125-$225.**

Bulova Accutron, 214 model back set.

Bulova 214, Accutron Anniversary Edition, gold-plate case, stainless back, designed in the shape of the Accutron tuning fork, Spaceview, **$395-$595.**

Bulova, Accutron model 214, circa 1974, railroad approved, **$395-$495.**

Cartier, Tank Automatique, circa 1970s, 18k, **$2,000-$3,000.**

Photo courtesy of Antiquorum.

Concord, circa 1940s, platinum and diamond, rose gold, ladies retro watch, **$2,500-$3,500.**

Corum, peacock feather, circa 1970s, 18k tank style, **$800-$1,000.**

Concord, circa 1940s, 14k, 17J, **$195-$395.**

Corum, Peacock Feather, circa 1970s, 18k, **$1,200-$2,400.**

Croton, "Pirate Buccaneer" back.

Croton, "Pirate Buccaneer," circa late 1940s to early 1950s, plated/stainless back, **$75-$150.**

Croton ladies, stainless
Croton automatic,
circa 1960s, GF, Nivada
Grenchen, circa 1950s,
$45-$95 each.

Swiss Croton, circa 1960s, sweep
seconds, stainless, **$75-$175.**

Cyma, with top closed.

Cyma, circa 1920s, sterling flip top push button, radium enamel dial, **$495-$795.**

Cyma, Tavannes 7J movement, circa WW I, nickel case-grill guard, **$195-$395.**

Cyma, circa 1920s, WGF 15J, GF, engraved bezel, **$95-$195.**

Elgin

Elgin, circa 1910s, GF, 15J, wire lug, **$95-$195.**

Lady Elgin, circa 1916 movement, GF, engraved edge, 1920s case, 15J, **$75-$150.**

Elgin, 15J movement.

Elgin, engraved
bezel style/base
metal, circa 1910s,
enamel dial blue
spade hands, 15J,
$95-$195.

Montgomery Bros., circa 1911, Elgin 15J movement, sterling-enamel dial, **$195-$495.**

Elgin, circa 1915, 15J, chrome engraved, radium hands and numerals, **$95-$195.**

Elgin, engraved
on back (Fremont
Whitney Ord. Dept.).

Elgin, military, circa
1917, nickel case, 7J,
heavy wire lugs-radium
hands, **$150-$450.**

Elgin, circa 1920s?,
7J, GF, rare case style,
$150-$300.

Elgin, circa 1918,
enamel dial, silver, wire
lug, **$150-$350.**

Ladies Elgin, circa
1921 movement.

Ladies Elgin, circa 1921, GF
15J, metal dial, **$75-$125.**

Elgin movement.

Elgin, circa 1918, 7J, watch band pins riveted on, GF, **$100-$250.**

Elgin, circa 1920s, 7J, enamel dial with sub seconds, GF swivel lugs, **$95-$195.**

Elgin, circa 1922, 15J, WGF case, engraved bezel edge, **$95-$195.**

Elgin, circa 1927, 14kt WG barrel-shaped case, large crown, 15J, **$75-$150.**

Elgin, circa 1929, 7J, WGF case, engraved bezel, **$75-$175.**

Elgin, circa 1930s, GF stepped case, **$95-$225.**

Elgin, Avigo, circa 1930s, 7J, chrome case, **$100-$250.**

Elgin, circa 1932, 7J, WGF engraved square case, **$100-$250.**

Elgin, circa 1933, curved case, hidden lugs, 7J, chrome case unusual design, **$100-$300.**

Elgin, mid-size, circa 1939, 15J, sweep second hand, **$75-$150.**

Elgin-movement and inside case back.

Elgin, circa 1930, GF, stepped engraved bezel, 7J, **$75-$150.**

Elgin, circa 1938, GF, stepped case, 15J, **$95-$195.**

Lord Elgin, circa 1940s, pink GF/two-tone dial, 21J, **$95-$225.**

Lord Elgin, driver's style black dial, circa 1950s, 21J, GF, **$100-$250.**

Lord Elgin, circa 1951, 21J, GF, **$75-$175.**

Lord Elgin, movement caliber 670.

Elgin, driver's watch, pink dial, circa 1950s, 21J, pink GF, **$100-$250.**

Elgin, circa 1951, GF, 17J, fancy lugs, **$95-$195.**

Lord Elgin, circa 1950s, gold filled, fancy hidden lugs, **$95-$195.**

Lord Elgin, circa 1950s, 21J, GF square case, **$95-$195.**

Elgin, circa 1950s, numerals on bezel, pinwheel dial, GF, **$95-$195.**

Elgin, circa 1952, 17J, GF, **$75-$175.**

Elgin, Lord Elgin digital, circa 1950s, 21J caliber movement, GF, **$400-$800.**

Elgin, 1950s, GF, textured dial, **$95-$195.**

Lord Elgin, circa 1950s, direct read-
with box, GF, **$495-$695.**

Elgin, money clip,
circa 1950s, 17J,
GF, **$95-$295.**

Ebel, ladies Swiss, circa
1960s, 14k with mesh
band, **$425-$625.**

Eska, circa 1941, mid-size early
self-winding, stainless, radium hands
sweep second, **$150-$250.**

Eterna, restored, circa 1940s, two-tone SS with gold lugs, **$195-$495.**

Eterna-Matic, "birks" 14k Centenaire "61," **$1,000-$1,500.**

Favre Leuba, alarm, circa 1960s, seabird, stainless, **$250-$450.**

Gelbros Swiss, circa 1920s, fancy engraved chrome case, radium hands, **$100-$200**.

Girard-Perregaux, Switzerland

Founded in the 1850s, this company is known to have been the first to produce wrist watches (1880s) for military use.

Girard Perregaux, "Sea Hawk," circa late 1940s,
stainless, two-tone dial, **$195-$395.**

Girard Perregaux, Gyromatic, chrome plated, 17J, **$95-$195.**

Girard Perregaux, Gyromatic, circa late 1950s-1960s, SS back/gold top/original dial, screw back, **$100-$250.**

Gruen Watch Co., Cincinnati, Ohio

Founded in the 1870s in Columbus, Ohio, Gruen is famous for its imported Swiss "Guild" movements, and for the "Veri-Thin," "Curvex," and "Doctors" watches.

Gruen Precision, ladies, circa 1920s, 14kt WG, diamond, **$395-$795.**

Gruen, circa 1930s, 17J, GF barrel shape, **$95-$195.**

Gruen Swiss, circa 1930, 15J, GF stepped case, **$95-$195.**

Gruen, Veri-Thin, circa 1940s, 24-hour military dial radium hands, GF, **$100-$250.**

Gruen, model 700, circa 1930s, 10k GF, 15J, restored dial, **$125.**

Gruen, Curvex Precision, circa 1940s, GF hooded lugs, 17J, **$195-$395**.

Gruen, ladies curvex, circa 1930s, GF, **$100-$250**.

Gruen, Precision,
circa 1950s, auto
wind/sweep second,
GF, **$75-$175.**

Gruen, Precision, auto-
wind, circa 1960s, day-
date, SS, **$75-$175.**

Group of ladies Gruen wrist watches, circa 1930s,
1940s and 1950s, **$50-$100 each.**

Gruen, Veri Thin Precision, circa 1940s, 14k, doctor's watch, **$795-$995.**

Gruen, Veri thin, circa 1945, 10k, GF, stainless back, 15J, **$95-$195.**

Gubelin, circa 1940s, restored/refinished dial, SS, original hands, **$100-$300**.

E. Gubelin, Swiss ladies, 14k, **$295-$395**.

Hamilton Watch Co.

Hamilton, square, circa 1923, green GF-enameled bezel, sub-seconds at 9:00, rare.

Hamilton, Piping Rock, circa 1928, 14kt white or yellow, enamel bezel, **$800-$1,400.**

Hamilton, circa 1930s, 17J
986 caliber, rare sub seconds
at 9:00, GF/early refinished
dial, **$200-$300.**

Hamilton, circa 1930s, 987A
movement, barrel shape,
17J, **$100-$200.**

Hamilton, Coronado, circa 1930s, 14kt WG swivel lugs, black enamel bezel, **$1,000-$2,400.**

Hamilton Coronado, closeup view.

Hamilton "Dixon," circa 1936, stepped lugs, applied numerals, 17J 987E movement, GF, **$100-$250.**

Hamilton Seckron, circa 1936, GF, doctor's watch, **$800-$1,300.**

Hamilton, "Gladstone,"
circa 1931, GF white,
17J, **$225-$425.**

Hamilton, "Gladstone"
movement/case back movement
is upgraded to 1940s, 987-F.

Hamilton, "Gladstone" engraved edge.

Hamilton Rutledge,
circa 1936, platinum,
$1,200-$2,500.

Hamilton Sidney, circa
1937, GF, **$100-$300.**

Hamilton Gilman, circa 1937,
14k, **$350-$700.**

Hamilton, Dodson, circa 1937,
17J, GF, **$100-$275.**

Hamilton, circa 1937
"Gilman," 14k/14k band,
$1,200-$1,800.

Hamilton "Brock," circa
1939, Grade 982, 14k, 19J,
$395-$795.

Hamilton, "Wilshire," circa 1939, pink GF, 19J, **$295-$495.**

Hamilton, circa 1940s, WGF, 17J 752 movement, applied numerals, **$100-$250.**

Hamilton, military
WW II, back of case.

Hamilton,
military WW II,
new-old stock,
$300-$400.

Hamilton "Martin," circa 1941, 987A movement, GF, **$100-$200.**

Hamilton, circa 1945, 14k diamond dial, hooded lugs, **$1,500-$2,000.**

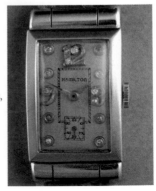

Hamilton, "Cambridge," circa 1949, platinum, **$1,100-$2,400.**

Hamilton ladies, square, diamond bezel, 14k, **$595-$995.**

Hamilton ladies watches: top: 22J WGF, circa 1950s; bottom: 17J "Peggy," circa 1940s, **$500-$100 each.**

Hamilton ladies, circa platinum/ diamond approximately 8ct total weight, **$7,000-$9,000.**

Hamilton "Brent," circa 1951, 14k GF 19J, **$175-$275.**

Hamilton, Transcontinental A, circa 1955, GF/time-zone dial, **$300-$750.**

Hamilton, electric "Van Horn," circa 1957, 14k, Shriner dial, **$395-$595.**

Hamilton, Victor Electric, circa 1957, GF, **$125-$375.**

Hamilton, Van Horn Electric, circa 1957, 14k, **$300-$500.**

Hamilton, Ventura Electric,
circa 1957, 14k yellow,
$1,200-$1,800.

Hamilton, Ventura Electric,
circa 1958, 14k white diamond
dial, **$3,000-$5,000.**

Hamilton, Ventura Electric, late 1950s, 18k pink gold, very rare.

Hamilton "Prentice," circa 1959, RGF, author's gold and rosewood band attached, **$95-$195.**

Hamilton, Regulus Electric, circa 1959, SS, **$300-$800.**

Hamilton "Thin-O-Matic" (rare), automatic, circa 1960, two-tone dial, GF, **$395-$695.**

Hamilton, Saturn
Electric, circa 1960,
GF, **$200-$500.**

Hamilton, Sherwood S, circa
1961, GF with teak dial and
band inserts, unusual.

Hamilton, Altair Electric,
circa 1962, GF, original band,
$1,800-$3,000.

Hamilton, Pacer Electric, circa
1958, GF, **$250-$750.**

Hamilton, Pacer Electric, circa late 1950s, corporate logo dial, **$300-$700.**

Hamilton Pacermatic (automatic movement), circa 1961, GF/rare, beware of fakes.

Hamilton, Savitar
Electric, circa 1962,
14k, **$350-$750.**

Hamilton, RR special electric,
circa 1963, 505 model,
stainless, **$175-$275.**

Hamilton Electric
Savitar II, GF, circa
1965, with company
logo, **$150-$400.**

Hamilton Electric
Taurus, circa 1962,
GF, **$100-$300.**

Hamilton, Vega Electric,
circa 1962, original band,
GF, **$800-$1,500.**

Hamilton, Victor II Electric,
circa 1962, GF, original
band, **$200-$500.**

Hamilton, K-475 Automatic, circa 1962, GF, extremely rare, **$2,000-$4,000.**

Hamilton, Polaris Electric, circa 1963, 14k, **$295-$495.**

Hamilton, circa 1960, 14k, **$350-$550.**

Hamilton automatic, circa 1960s, sweep second hand, stainless, **$150-$250.**

Hamilton automatic, circa 1960s, stainless sweep second hand, **$150-$250.**

Hamilton, T-403 Automatic, two-tone dial with date, circa 1965, GF, **$395-$695.**

Hamilton, Lord Lancaster J Electric, circa 1965, GF/diamond dial, **$300-$700.**

Hamilton, Odyssee 2001 Automatic, circa 1969, date at 6:00, SS, **$500-$900.**

Hamilton Vesta, ladies
version of the Altair,
original box, GF,
$300-$700.

Hamilton LED Digital,
circa 1970s, stainless/
screw back, original
band, **$195-$295.**

Hilton, circa 1950s, stainless, 17J-manual wind, **$75-$150.**

Helbros, circa 1940s, silver cased black dial sweep second, **$95-$195.**

Helbros, ladies Art Deco,
circa 1930s, 15J WGF, fancy
engraved case, **$45-$95.**

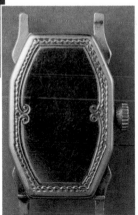

Helbros, ladies Art Deco back.

Illinois Watch Co., Springfield,
circa 1918, sterling, 15J,
$495-$795.

Illinois Watch Co.,
movement view.

Ingersoll, circa 1920s, base metal, inexpensive early wrist watch, **$50-$100.**

Ingraham USA (2), circa 1940s, original crystal yellowed with age, 0 jewel, **$25-$75 each.**

Helbros, circa 1950s, 14k
case, diamond dial at 12, 3,
and 9, 17J, **\$125-\$275.**

International Watch Co.,
circa 1940s, platinum,
\$5,000-\$7,000.

Photo courtesy of
Antiquorum.

Jaeger-Le Coultre, Switzerland

This fine company dates back to 1833 when Antoine Le Coultre established his watchmaking workshop in Le Sentier, Switzerland. In 1847, Le Coultre produced its first movement with a crown winding and setting system, eliminating the need for watch keys. In 1903, the company unveiled the world's flattest pocket watch caliber, and at 1.38 mm thick, it remains an unbroken record.

In 1925, tiny Art Deco watches were created, featuring the twin-level rectangular Duoplan movement, that were way ahead of their time in terms of accurate timekeeping. In 1929, Le Coultre reduced the mechanical watch movement to its smallest dimension ever—caliber 101. Measuring 14 x 4.8 x 3.4 mm, comprising 98 parts, and weighing around one gram, it is still the world's smallest mechanical movement and is still in production.

In 1931, the company met the challenge to build a watch rugged enough to be worn in sporting events by inventing the Reverso. This wrist watch, with a swivel case, turns its back on shocks to protect the fragile glass. It is one of the few remaining authentic Art Deco creations still being produced. In 1953, Jaeger-LeCoultre developed the Futurematic. This watch is equipped with a power-reserve indicator and is the first automatic watch to require no winding crown. In 1956, the first automatic alarm wrist watch was created, the Memovox. The company still makes fabulous mechanical watches to this day in Le Sentier. The following photos are courtesy of Jaeger-LeCoultre.

Queen Elizabeth II wore the Jaeger-LeCoultre
calibre 101 on her coronation day.

Drivers' style watches, with crown at 6 o' clock.

The Duoplan, circa 1925, with a split-level movement.

The first Reverso, circa 1931, the legendary swivel watch.

LeCoultre Reverso, circa 1930s, 18k, **$7,000-$9,000.**

Photo courtesy of Antiquorum.

Jaeger-LeCoultre
Memovox, circa 1956,
the first automatic
wrist-watch alarm.

LeCoultre, Master
Mariner automatic,
circa 1950s, power wind
indicator, GF stainless
back, **$195-$495.**

LeCoultre alarm, circa
1950s, raised numerals,
stainless, **$295-$595.**

Jaeger LeCoultre,
Mysterieuse, circa
1960s, 18k white,
$2,800-$3,500.

Photo courtesy of
Antiquorum.

Longines, Switzerland

Founded in 1867, Longines became the world's first watch trademark and the first Swiss company to assemble watches under one roof. In 1877, Longines won the first of its 10 World's Fair grand prizes and 28 gold medals, and it was the beginning of Longines' rightful claim to the title of "The World's Most Honored Watch." In 1899, the Duke of Abbruzi completed a successful Arctic Ocean expedition with Longines chronometers used as instrumentation. In 1927, Colonel Charles Lindbergh completed a first non-stop flight from New York to Paris using a Longines watch for time and instrumentation. From 1928 through 1938, the likes of Admiral Byrd, Amelia Earhart, Howard Hughs, Von Schiller, captain of the "Graf Zeppelin," and other adventurers placed their trust in Longines watches. In 1953, Longines developed the first quartz movement. Stainless steel automatics from the 1950s and 1960s are highly collectible, as are the early Longines wrist watches from the 1910s and 1920s.

Handmade 14k gold and rosewood watchband,
with vintage 1955 Longines, **$1,500.**
Note: Rosewood band made by author.

A 1934 metal toy truck, pictured with the author's 1912 Longines wrist watch.

Longines, circa 1912, enamel dial/Roman numerals, sterling wire lug case, 15J, **$195-$395.**

Longines, ladies, circa mid-1920s, GF wire lugs, enamel bezel, 15J, **$125-$225.**

Longines, ladies.
1920s movement.

Longines, circa 1920s, sterling with solid lugs, enamel dial, **$150-$350.**

Longines, circa 1937, 17J GF, **$195-$295.**

Longines, circa
1940s, 14k curved,
$395-$695.

Longines, ladies, circa 1940s, 14k WG,
fancy diamond case, **$495-$795.**

Longines, circa 1940s, 14k multicolored pink and green 17J faceted crystal, **$1,500-$2,000.**

Longines, circa 1949, 14k gold, manual wind, **$195-$595.**

Longines, circa late 1940s
early 1950s, flared case,
17J, 14k, **$395-$595.**

Longines, circa 1950s,
hour-glass case, 17J GF,
$395-$595.

Longines, circa 1950s, 14k, fancy lugs, faceted crystal, **$395-$695.**

Longines automatic, circa 1950s, 17J GF, original dial, **$195-$295.**

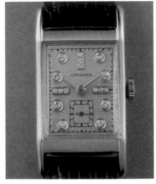

Longines, circa 1950,
14k white-diamond dial,
$1,295-$1,695.

Longines, circa 1952,
17J, GF, **$100-$250.**

Longines, circa 1951,
14k sub seconds,
$195-$495.

Longines, Ultra Chron,
circa 1960s, Auto/ Date/
SS, **$295-$495.**

Longines, circa 1960s,
14k, white sub seconds,
$195-$395.

Longines, automatic with
date, circa 1970s, stainless
gray dial, **$295-$395.**

Circa 1919 "Tonneau" style, enamel dial/Breguet style numerals, silver/935.

Photo courtesy Longines Museum Collection.

Circa 1912, 14k white gold case set with diamonds, 12 painted Breguet style numerals, external minute track.

Photo courtesy Longines Museum Collection.

Lucien Piccard, ladies diamond and ruby, 14k rose, **$895-$1,295.**

Lucien Piccard, ladies bracelet watch, 14k multicolored green and pink faceted crystal, **$495-$795.**

Lucien Piccard, Swiss automatic day date, GP, stainless back, **$75-$175.**

Marvin Watch Co.-Swiss, circa 1942, radium hands sub seconds, base metal, mirror effect on dial, **$50-$125.**

Mido, multifort automatic, circa 1940s, stainless, mid-size, **$75-$175.**

Mido, multifort, circa 1950s, super automatic power wind, stainless, **$75-$175.**

Moser Longines Omega, large oversized pocket watches converted to wrist watches, circa 1910s, **$295-$595.**

Moser Longines Omega, all three movements of watches pictured above.

Movado Museum, circa 1976,
14k, **$2,000-$3,000.**

Movado, close up of the Chronograph's 17J Swiss movement.

Movado, Tiffany & Co., Chronograph, circa 1940s, 14k, **$1,500-$2,500.**

Photo courtesy of Antiquorum.

Movado, circa 1914, white gold
half moon-shaped case.

Photo courtesy of Movado Watch Co.

Movado, ladies, circa 1960s,
14k gold with mesh band,
extra small, **$695-$895.**

Ulysse Nardin, vintage wrist repeater, estimated value is **$25,000- $40,000**.

Photo courtesy of Ulysse Nardin.

Early cushion-shaped Movado lady's watch, in 18k, made in 1915.

Photo courtesy of Movado Watch Co.

Omega, Switzerland

This prolific company first started producing watches in 1848 and is famed for its timing of the Olympics for decades. In 1969, Neil Armstrong stepped onto the lunar surface wearing an Omega Speedmaster Professional, the only watch ever worn on the moon, and to this day the only watch issued to every NASA astronaut. Omega watches are very collectible, especially the "Seamaster" and the "Constellation" automatic models, as well as any of its Chronographs.

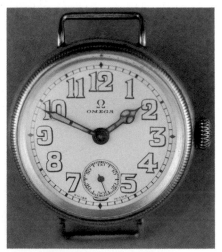

Omega, circa 1910, silver round wire
lug, enamel dial, **$495-$695.**

Omega (very rare), minute repeater, circa 1892.
Photo courtesy of Omega.

Omega, chronograph shown with movement, circa 1913, wire lug case.
Photo courtesy of Omega.

Omega, half hunter-demi-hunter, circa 1899, double-pointed hour hand-two dials, estimated at **$1,500-$2,500.**

Photo courtesy of Omega.

Omega, military, circa 1916, steel case with protective grill, caliber 13 movement, estimated at **$295-$595.**

Photo courtesy of Omega.

Omega chronograph
caliber 39, circa 1929,
gold button at 6,
estimated at **$3,000-
$5,000.**

Photo courtesy of
Omega.

Omega,
chronograph,
circa 1932,
stainless, estimated
at **$2,000-
$4,000.**

Photo courtesy
of Omega.

Omega, circa 1936, 15J-manual wind, black dial roman numerals, **$195-$395.**

Omega, chronograph military, circa 1937, stainless, estimated at **$1,500-$2,500.**

Photo courtesy of Omega.

Omega, left: stainless steel Chronograph, circa 1940; right: wire lug Chronograph, circa 1924.

Photo courtesy of Omega.

Omega, British watch ad, featuring the caliber 30.

It is not generally appreciated that in spite of Germany's occupation of every surrounding country, Switzerland did supply Great Britain with all the goods needed and ordered for the war effort. And we needed and ordered a lot.

To give only one instance: as every Airman knows, all the Navigational watches used by the R.A.F. during the war were made in Switzerland. Approximately half of these were

OMEGA
WATCHES

OMEGA WATCH CO. (ENGLAND) LTD.
24-30 HOLBORN VIADUCT, LONDON, E.C.1.
Makers of precision watches since 1848.

Omega, Chronometer, circa 1940s, pink gold, rare, **$900-$1,800.**

Omega, square button chronograph, circa 1946, 18k pink, **$1,000-$2,000.**

Photo courtesy of Antiquorum.

Omega, military-RAF (Royal Air Force), circa 1950s, stainless, black dial, **$250-$750.**

Omega-Areo, oversized, 1950s airplane sub-seconds at 9, two-tone gold with black dial, base metal-pocket watch movement, **$250-$500.**

Omega Automatic, circa 1951, 18k, **$1,300-$1,800.**

Photo courtesy of Antiquorum.

Omega, early 1950 automatic-wind movement, caliber 455.

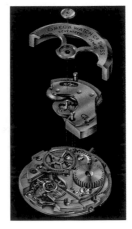

This Omega Art Deco ad dedicated the arrival of the caliber 20 that was launched in 1929.

Omega, Ranchero, circa 1958, rare, stainless, ultra anti-magnetic, **$1,500-$2,500.**

Omega, circa 1950,
18J 14k, flared lugs,
$1,200-$1,500.

Omega automatic,
circa 1950s, stainless/
original mesh band,
$395-$695.

Omega Early
Speedmaster,
Chronograph, circa 1957,
stainless with black dial,
$1,500-$2,500.

Photo courtesy of Omega.

Omega, Geneve, circa 1960s,
automatic date, stainless,
$125-$275.

Omega, Speedmaster
Professional, three register
chronograph, circa 1966, 17J
stainless, **$1,000-$1,500.**

Omega, Speedmaster
Professional, Chronograph,
approved by NASA, stainless,
$900-$1,400.

Omega bracelet watch, circa 1969, 14k with 14k bracelet, 17J, **$395-$595.**

Omega Automatic, circa 1963, 18k, **$1,000-$1,500.**

Photo courtesy of Antiquorum.

Case back view Observatory.

Omega Constellation, Automatic Chronometer Date, circa 1970s, stainless, **$295-$495.**

Omega, SS clasp and band.

Omega, circa 1973, Seamaster DeVille stainless, SS Omega band, **$250-$500.**

Omega, Seamaster
DeVille case back.

Omega, pair of Seamaster DeVilles.

Patek Philippe, made for Tiffany & Co., circa 1925, 18k cushion shape, **$9,000-$11,000.**

Photo courtesy of Antiquorum.

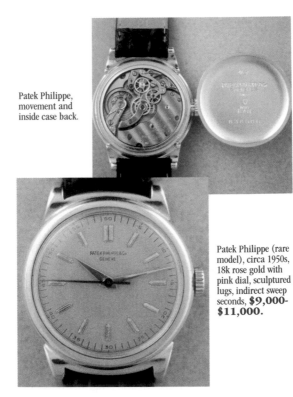

Patek Philippe, movement and inside case back.

Patek Philippe (rare model), circa 1950s, 18k rose gold with pink dial, sculptured lugs, indirect sweep seconds, **$9,000-$11,000.**

Patek Philippe, contract case 18k, converted pendant to wrist watch, dial refinished, **$2,500.**

Philippe Calatrava (rare), original dial-manual wind, circa 1955, stainless-WP case, **$7,000-$12,000.**

Patek Philippe movement.

Patek Philippe, Geneve
for Tiffany & Co., circa
approximately 1964, 18k,
18J, **$3,000-$4,500.**

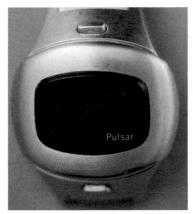

Pulsar LED, Time Computer Inc. USA,
circa 1970s, stainless, **$100-$300.**

Piaget, bracelet watch, circa 1960s,
18k, **$1,600-$2,000.**

Photo courtesy of Antiquorum.

Rolex, Switzerland

When Rolex started producing the first truly waterproof watch, the "Rolex Oyster," in the later half of the 1920s, it has forever since been associated with high quality and durability. Watch collector connoisseurs love their Rolex, for they know that long after the price is forgotten, the quality remains.

Rolex, ladies, circa 1922, 14k pink round diamond bezel, **$1,500-$2,000.**

Precision, circa 1940s, 18k with diamond-set bracelet, **$2,000-$3,000.**

Photo courtesy of Antiquorum.

Rolex Oyster, Chronometre Observatory, circa 1941, stainless, **$2,200-$2,600.**

Rolex circa 1944, chronometer,
14k pink, **$1,500-$2,000.**

Rolex, circa 1920s,
mid-size sterling
silver case, 15J,
blue enamel bezel,
$1,500-$2,000.

Rolex, Viceroy, circa 1930s, stainless case with pink bezel, manual wind, **$1,200-$2,400.**

Rolex, Oyster Bubble Back, circa 1940s, silver California dial, stainless, **$2,000-$4,000.**

Rolex, Oyster Raleigh,
Ref. #2784, circa 1940s,
stainless, **$500-$700.**

Rolex ladies, circa 1940s to
1950s, 18k with 18k band,
$2,500-$3,500.

Rolex Oyster Royalite, circa 1942, stainless, **$1,250-$1,750.**

Rolex Oyster, circa 1940s, stainless bubble back, refinished dial, **$900-$1,400.**

Rolex, circa 1940s, 14k pink stainless back, 17J, hooded lugs, **$1,500-$2,000.**

Rolex, Datejust, circa 1950, rare alternate red and black date, 18k pink gold case with black dial, **$3,500-$5,500.**

Rolex, Datejust, circa 1953, 14k gold and stainless case, alternate red/black date, **$2,000-$2,500.**

Rolex, ref. #6234, Chronograph 72A, circa 1950s, rare, stainless-original dial, **$11,000-$14,000.**

Rolex, ref. #6234, Chronograph, circa 1950s, 14k gold case, luminous markers and hands, **$18,000-$20,000.**

Rolex Oyster Perpetual, ref. #6536, submariner (earliest sub), circa 1950s, indicator on rotating bezel missing, **$3,000-$4,000.**

Rolex Explorer, ref. #1016, circa 1950s, stainless, **$3,000-$4,000.**

Rolex, GMT Master ref #6542, circa 1955, blue and red bezel, stainless, **$2,500-$5,000.**

Rolex Oyster Perpetual, ref. #6565, circa 1955, stainless, **$1,750-$2,250.**

Rolex, circa late 1950s, 18k, Bomb'e lugs, **$2,500-$3,000.**

Rolex, ref 6634, gold top over stainless backing, two-tone case, **$750-$1,050.**

Rolex, circa 1950s, 14k, **$2,200-$2,700.**

Rolex, ladies, with diamonds,
circa 1950, 14k white,
$2,000-$2,500.

Rolex Oyster Perpetual,
stainless, circa 1958,
$1,400-$1,800.

Rolex, Oyster Perpetual, circa
1959, two tone/smooth bezel,
$1,500-$2,000.

Rolex Oyster, circa
1950s, stainless, unusual
large sub seconds,
$1,000-$1,500.

Rolex Tudor, Oyster Prince, circa late 1950s/1960s, self-winding, stainless, **$295-$495.**

Rolex, Queen Midas, circa 1960s, 18k midsize, **$3,500-$4,500.**

Photo courtesy of Antiquorum.

Rolex Oyster Perpetual, ref. #5512, Submariner, circa 1960s, stainless, **$2,500-$3,500.**

Rolex Oyster Perpetual, GMT Master, ref. #1675, circa 1968, stainless, **$2,000-$3,000.**

Rolex Oyster Precision, circa 1970, stainless case with pink dial, **$1,000-$1,450.**

Rolex, Ladies Oyster Date, Ref. 6917, 18k, **$2,000-$3,000.**

Rolex, circa late
1960s/early 1970s,
diamond dial, stainless,
$1,200-$1,700.

Rolex, Datejust Ref 1625,
circa late 1960s/early 1970s,
stainless, Thunderbird bezel,
$2,500-$3,000.

Rolex ladies, Perpetual,
18k, black dial sub seconds,
$1,500-$2,000.

Rolex Oyster Perpetual,
Milgauss Chronometer,
circa 1970s, stainless-ref.
#1019, ultra anti-magnetic,
$9,000-$12,000.

Rolex Oyster Cosmograph,
Daytona, ref. #6263,
circa 1970s, stainless,
$9,000-$12,000.

Rolex Oyster Date, stainless,
$900-$1,200.

Seiko, circa 1930s, 7J chrome, Hermetic case within case, **$395-$595.**

Seiko, automatic day date, circa 1970s, blue dial, stainless, **$75-$150.**

Seiko, automatic day date, circa 1970s, two-tone dial, stainless, **$75-$150.**

Seiko Chronograph, automatic day date, circa 1970s, stainless, **$150-$300.**

Shreve & Co., high-grade Swiss movement.

Shreve & Co., high grade Swiss movement, 18k, wire lug/enamel dial, **$600-$1,000.**

Tavannes, circa 1942, GF 17J, **$95-$195.**

Tavannes, Art Deco 1920s, 14k rose gold massive curved case, gold dial with exploding numerals, made for Russian market, **$1,500-$2,000.**

Tissot, Switzerland

Started in 1853, Charles F. Tissot founded a small watch factory in Le Locle, Switzerland. Tissot supplied watches to Russia and the "Tsar's Court." This fine company merged with the Omega Watch Co. in 1929 and still produced a line of quality watches to the present day. The company has produced many fine wrist watches and pocket watches, including chronometer escapements. The following photos are courtesy of Tissot.

Early Tissot parts box.

Tissot, Chronograph, circa late 1930s, stainless swivel lugs, **$1,300-$2,000.**

Tissot ladies, circa 1960s, gold top plated stainless back, 17J, **$45-$95.**

0 size Betsy Ross movement, HC movement made into wristwatch.

US Watch Co. of Waltham, circa early 1900s movement, chrome 0 size Betsy Ross, **$95-$195.**

Tissot, Navigator, circa 1953, world time, automatic, stainless, **$1,000-$1,500.**

Wakmann, three-register Chronograph, circa 1940s, stainless, **$250-$500.**

Waltham, circa 1910s,
base metal case with metal
dial, blue spade hands,
15J, **$95-$145.**

Waltham, circa 1930, 15J
"sapphire" movement, ribbed
case near lugs, yellowed
crystal, **$50-$125.**

Waltham, 17J "Ruby" movement.

Waltham, circa 1934, GF, 17J "Ruby" movement, **$100-$200.**

Waltham, circa 1915, GF, wire lug enamel dial, rare offset face, **$700-$1,100.**

Waltham, circa 1937, GF, 17J Crescent St. movement, **$100-$225.**

Waltham, circa 1950, GF-black dial, 25J, **$100-$250.**

Waltham, Incabloc Swiss, circa late 1950s, GF 17J, sub-seconds, **$45-$95.**

Zenith movement.

Zenith, William Farmer & Co. LTD, Sydney, circa 1920s, Swiss 17J, wire lug, **$150-$350.**

Welsbro, asymmetrical, GF, ladies
Swiss, 1950s, **$95-$150.**

Wittnauer, circa 1970s,
day date/manual wind,
unusual blue dial
with years, stainless,
$175-$275.

Wittnauer, circa 1940s,
sub-seconds automatic,
GF, **$95-$195.**

Wittnauer, ladies watch movement.

Wittnauer, ladies, circa 1960s, 14kt case GF band, **$100-$200.**

Wyler, Chronograph,
circa 1940s, stainless,
$395-$795.

Wyler, circa 1940s,
stainless-Incaflex, sub-
seconds, **$95-$195.**

Universal Aero-Compax, chronograph,
square pushers 18k, **$3,000-$4,000.**

Waltham 1916 movement.

Waltham, circa 1916, 15J
enamel dial, sterling wire
lug, **$195-$295.**

Vacheron Constantin, automatic, circa 1970s, 18k white, **$3,000-$4,000.**

Photo courtesy of Antiquorum.

Vacheron Constantin, circa 1954, 18k pink rare-style case, **$4,000-$6,000.**

Photo courtesy of Antiquorum.

Universal Geneve, Compax
Chronograph, circa 1960s,
$900-$1,200.

Photo courtesy of Antiquorum.

Vacheron Constantin,
automatic, circa 1966, 18k,
$2,000-$3,000.

Photo courtesy of Antiquorum.

Waltham, circa 1934, 17J, engraved edge, white rolled gold plate, **$75-$150.**

Waltham Curvex style, GF, circa 1936, 17J 50mm lug to lug, **$295-$395.**

Waltham, circa late 1950s/
early 1060s, alarm, 17J date,
stainless, **$295-$495.**

Waltham, circa late
1950s/early 1960s, 21J,
self-winding, stainless,
$95-$195.

Asymmetrical, circa 1950s ladies Swiss, GF, 17J, **$95-$150.**

Waltham Premier, circa 1940s, RGP, 17J, **$45-$95.**

Wittnauer, Automatic day date, circa late 1960s/early 1970s, stainless with hacking feature, **$95-$195.**

Miscellaneous Swiss

Swiss pendant watch, geometric Art Deco back.

Swiss pendant watch, circa 1920s, Art Deco, blue, purple, and green enamel, geometric design, **$95-$225.**

Swiss, circa 1910s, pin set onion crown, radium black dial, wire lug, **$600-$800.**

Swiss, circa 1910s, silver wire lug, radium dial and hands, **$150-$350.**

Swiss wire lug
case back.

Swiss, pin
set-wire lug,
silver and gold
engraved case
back, enamel
dial, **$295-
$595.**

Swiss, circa 1910,
silver wire lug, Roman
numerals, **$95-$195.**

Swiss Civic, circa
1918, enamel dial
wire lug, nickel,
$395-$695.

Back view.

Ladies, 14k wire lug,
circa 1918, exploded
numbers, **$125-$225.**

Swiss Buren "Tribune,"
circa 1920s, wire lug
enamel bezel, 15J 14k,
$150-$250.

Swiss Solrey Watch Co., circa 1920s,
WGF radium hands and numerals,
engraved bezel, **$95-$195.**

Hansel Sloan and Co., high-grade Swiss movement.

Hansel Sloan and Co., Swiss, circa 1920s, silver/enamel dial, **$350-$500.**

Swiss, circa 1920s,
sterling case with wire
lugs, **$250-$450.**

F. De Ferrari & Co., San
Francisco, CA, circa 1920s,
sterling enamel dial, roman
numerals, **$150-$350.**

Swiss Medana group, circa 1920s, wire lug wristwatches, **$50-$95 each.**

Group of six Swiss mid-sized ladies watches, circa 1910s-1920s, silver wire lug enamel dials, **$75-$150 each.**

Swiss Westfield, circa 1930s-1940s, 7J GF, **$75-$150.**

Swiss Reflex, circa 1930s, early waterproof watch, stainless, **$295-$595.**

Time Square pin-watch back.

Swiss Time Square, circa 1930s, pin-back watch, sterling silver-Helbros movement, rubies-diamonds, **$250-$500.**

Swiss, ladies, circa 1940, 14k rose gold case and band, copper dial, **$550-$950.**

Swiss Rima, bracelet watch, circa 1940s, GF, 1-inch wide engraved band, **$95-$195.**

Group of four Swiss ladies watches, wire lug, **$40-$95.**

Rulon, circa 1940s, .750 total weight diamonds, platinum, fancy bracelet band, **$900-$1,250.**

Swiss Abercrombie & Fitch Co., Chronograph, circa 1940s, stainless, **$600-$1,000.**

Swiss Glycine in box.

Swiss Glycine, ladies bracelet watch, diamond and emerald, platinum 17J, **$4,000-$6,000.**

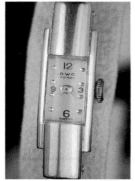

Swiss BWC, bracelet watch,
18k pink, **$595-$795.**

Swiss Ladies, seed pearls
and turquoise around bezel,
9k high-grade Swiss pin
set, **$1,200-$1,800.**

Swiss Chalet ladies, 14k pink and white, 17J, **$75-$175.**

Swiss, circa 1940s, rubies and diamonds unusual case, 14k pink, **$900-$1,400.**

Rona Sport Chronograph, circa 1940s, black metal mtg, for auto/plane, **$900-$1,200.**

Midland day date, circa late 1940s early 1950s, 17J, stainless, **$95-$195.**

Swiss "Louis," circa 1940s, GP 7J, stainless back, **$75-$125.**

Henry Blac, circa 1930s, silver case jump hour, Art Deco, **$2,000-$3,000.**

Photo courtesy of Antiquorum.

Fancy enamel cherub and floral watch stand, circa
1880, holds small ladies cylinder watch, **$700.**

Avia, automatic, circa 1970s, stainless, Digital Jump Hour, **$95-$145.**

Texas Instruments, LED, circa 1970s, anodized base metal case, **$95-$195.**

Swiss "Daniels," circa late 1940s, 17J, stainless sweep second, **$60-$120.**

Swiss "Belca," circa 1950s, stainless/manual wind, **$40-$75.**

Swiss Sinsa Sport, pin lever, base metal, stop-watch function only, no return to zero function, **$45-$95.**

Swiss Rogers, precision technician, circa 1960, 17J plated/stainless back, **$75-$120.**

Swiss Dufonte, automatic by Lucien Piccard, circa late 1960s to early 1970s, GP with stainless back, **$75-$150.**

Swiss Digital Mechanical, Custom Time, circa 1960s to 1970s, large oversize base metal stainless back, **$75-$175.**

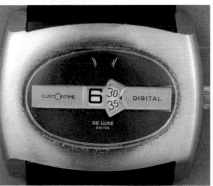

Leora Swiss, lapel watch, GP with enamel back, **$75-$175.**

Leora enamel case back.

Button-hole watch, side view.

Swiss Button Hole Watch, gun metal and enamel with cylinder movement, **$95-$195.**

Pendant watch back view.

Pendant, 14k, high-relief carved case with diamonds, high-grade Swiss movement, enamel dial, **$1,500-$2,500.**

Cartier France Art Deco purse attachment, exotic skin and tortoise shell, back wind and set 18k, **$4,000-$6,000.**

Cartier free standing.

Pendant watch ornate top.

Pendant watch hanging.

Swiss Ball pendant watch, round enameled, circa 1920s, turquoise enamel gold accents, matching chain, **$95-$225.**

Character Watches

Character watch, U.S. time, circa 1940s, Mickey Mouse, steel case, original red band, **$95-$195.**

Ingersoll, character watch, Mickey Mouse, circa 1930s, steel case, original band, paper dial-sub seconds, **$250-$750.**

Character watch, Dick
Tracy, circa 1940s,
stainless, **$125-$325.**

Character watch,
Honest Time Co.,
Nixon, circa 1970s,
eyes move side
to side as it ticks,
$75-$175.

Hopalong Cassidy, in original box with saddle, steel case, character watch, **$495-$595**.

Hopalong Cassidy watch, back of case engraved "Good Luck from Hoppy."

Character watch, Hopalong Cassidy, U.S. time, steel case, **$50-$200**.

Hopalong Cassidy in box, U.S. Time Corp., circa approx. 1950s, PW OF, **$150-$550.**

Original Hopalong Cassidy box.

Production Numbers and Dates

Here are approximate production numbers and dates of various watch companies (source: American Watchmakers-Clockmakers Institute):

Ansonia
1910	1,000,000
1915	3,000,000
1920	5,000,000
1925	7,000,000
1930	10,000,000

Auburndale
1880	3,000
1885	9,000

Aurora
1885	60,000
1886	110,000
1887	160,000
1888	200,000
1889	215,000

Ball
Made in Elgin, Waltham, Hamilton, and Illinois factories, which accounts for more than one series of numbers.
1900	60,701
	420,000
1905	202,001
	462,000
1910	216,201
	600,000

1915	250,000
	603,000
1920	260,000
	610,000
1925	270,000
1928	800,000
1930	801,000
	637,000
1931	803,000
1935	641,000
1938	647,000
1939	650,000
1940	651,000
1941	652,000
1942	654,000

Bannatyne Watch Co.
1906	40,000
1908	140,000
1910	250,000

Bulova
On the back of many Bulova watchcases are letters and numbers indicating the year of manufacture.
1946	46
1947	47
1948	4B

1949	J9
1950	L0
1951	L1
1952	L2
1953	L3
1954	L4
1955	L5
1956	L6
1957	L7
1958	L8
1959	L9
1960	M0
1961	M1
1962	M2
1963	M3
1964	M4
1965	M5
1966	M6
1967	M7
1968	M8
1969	M9
1970	N0
1971	N1
1972	N2
1973	N3
1974	N4

Cheshire
1890	50,000
1895	100,000

Columbus
1883	20,000
1884	50,000
1885	80,000
1886	100,000
1887	130,000
1888	160,000
1889	190,000
1890	225,000
1891	250,000
1892	275,000
1893	300,000
1894	340,000
1895	355,000
1896	380,000
1897	400,000
1898	415,000
1899	435,000
1900	460,000
1901	475,000
1902	485,000
1903	500,000

Dudley Watch Co.
Dudley Watch Co., 1920-1925
	500-2,000

P. W. Baker Co., 1925-1935
	2,001-4,800

XL Watch Co., 1935-

1976 4,801-6,500	

Elgin

1867 101	
1870 100,000	
1872 200,000	
1874 300,000	
1875 400,000	
1877 500,000	
1879 600,000	
1880 700,000	
1881 800,000	
1882 900,000	
1884 1,000,000	
1885 1,800,000	
1886 2,0000	
1888 3,000,000	
1890 4,000,000	
1893 5,000,000	
1895 6,000,000	
1897 7,000,000	
1899 8,000,000	
1900 9,000,000	
1903 10,000,000	
1904 11,000,000	
1905 12,000,000	
1907 13,000,000	
1909 14,000,000	
1910 15,000,000	
1911 16,000,000	
1912 17,000,000	
1914 18,000,000	
1916 19,000,000	
1917 20,000,000	
1918 21,000,000	
1919 22,000,000	
1920 23,000,000	
1921 24,000,000	
1922 25,000,000	
1923 26,000,000	
1924 27,000,000	

1925 28,000,000	
1926 29,000,000	
1927 30,000,000	
1928 31,000,000	
1929 32,000,000	
1930 33,000,000	
1933 34,000,000	
1934 35,000,000	
1936 36,000,000	
1938 37,000,000	
1939 38,200,000	
1940 39,100,000	
1941 40,200,000	
1942 41,100,000	
1943 42,200,000	
1945 43,200,000	
1947 45,000,000	
1948 46,000,000	
1949 47,000,000	
1950 48,000,000	
1951 49,000,000	
1952 50,000,000	

Charles Fasoldt Watch Co.

1855-1864 5-80	
1865-1868 90-161	
1868-1878 .. 335-540	

Hamilton

1893 1,000	
1894 5,000	
1895 10,000	
1896 14,000	
1897 20,000	
1898 30,000	
1899 40,000	
1900 50,000	
1901 90,000	
1902 150,000	
1903 260,000	

1904 340,000	
1905 425,000	
1906 590,000	
1907 756,000	
1908 921,000	
1909 1,050,000	
1910 1,087,000	
1911 1,290,000	
1912 1,331,000	
1913 1,370,000	
1914 1,410,000	
1915 1,450,000	
1916 1,517,000	
1917 1,580,000	
1918 1,650,000	
1919 1,700,000	
1920 1,790,000	
1921 1,860,000	
1922 1,900,000	
1923 1,950,000	
1924 2,000,000	
1925 2,100,000	
1926 2,200,000	
1927 2,250,000	
1928 2,300,000	
1929 2,350,000	
1930 2,400,000	
1931 2,450,000	
1932 2,500,000	
1933 2,600,000	
1934 2,700,000	
1935 2,800,000	
1936 2,900,000	
1937 3,000,000	
1938 3,200,000	
1939 3,400,000	
1940 3,600,000	
1941 3,800,000	
1942 4,025,000	

Hampden

1875 40,000	
1877 60,000	
1878 91,000	
1879 122,000	
1880 153,000	
1881 184,000	
1882 215,000	
1883 250,000	
1884 300,000	
1885 350,000	
1886 400,000	
1887 450,000	
1888 500,000	
1889 555,500	
1890 611,000	
1891 666,500	
1892 722,000	
1893 775,000	
1894 833,000	
1895 888,500	
1896 944,000	
1897 1,000,000	
1898 1,128,000	
1899 1,256,000	
1900 1,384,000	
1901 1,512,000	
1902 1,642,000	
1903 1,768,000	
1904 1,896,000	
1905 2,024,000	
1906 2,152,000	
1907 2,280,000	
1908 2,408,000	
1909 2,536,000	
1910 2,664,000	
1911 2,792,000	
1912 2,920,000	
1913 3,048,000	
1914 3,176,000	

1915 3,304,000	1886 340,000	1927 5,000,000	1923 62,000,000
1916 3,432,000	1887 350,000	(Company sold	1924 65,000,000
1917 3,560,000	1888 360,000	to Hamilton)	1925 67,500,000
1918 3,680,000	1889 380,000	1928 5,200,000	1926 69,000,000
1919 3,816,000	1890 400,000	1929 5,350,000	1927 70,500,000
1920 3,944,000	1891 430,000	1930 5,400,000	1928 71,500,000
1921 4,072,000	1892 460,000	1931 5,500,000	1929 73,500,000
1922 4,200,000	1893 470,000	1932 5,600,000	1930 75,000,000
1923 4,400,000	1894 525,000		
1924 4,600,000	1895 590,000	**Ingersoll**	**E. Ingraham**
	1896 650,000	1892 150,000	1905 50,000
Howard	1897 700,000	1893 310,000	1910 250,000
1859 20,000	1898 850,000	1894 650,000	1915 2,000,000
1860 44,000	1899 900,000	1895 1,000,000	1920 4,000,000
1870 200,000	1900 1,300,000	1896 2,000,000	1925 7,000,000
1880 550,000	1902 1,500,000	1897 2,900,000	1930 10,000,000
1890 700,000	1903 1,650,000	1898 3,500,000	
1900 850,000	1904 1,700,000	1899 3,750,000	**Lancaster**
1909 980,000	1905 1,800,000	1900 6,000,000	1880 50,000
1912 1,100,000	1906 1,840,000	1901 6,700,000	1885 100,000
1915 1,285,000	1907 1,900,000	1902 7,200,000	1890 150,000
1917 1,340,000	1908 2,100,000	1903 7,900,000	
1921 1,400,000	1909 2,150,000	1904 8,100,000	**A. Lange &**
1930 1,500,000	1910 2,200,000	1905 10,000,000	**Sohne**
	1911 2,300,000	1906 12,500,000	1870 1,500
Illinois	1912 2,400,000	1907 15,000,000	1875 10,000
1872	1913 2,500,000	1908 17,500,000	1880 20,000
First watch made	1914 2,600,000	1909 20,000,000	1885 25,000
1873 20,000	1915 2,700,000	1910 25,000,000	1890 30,000
1874 50,000	1916 2,800,000	1911 30,000,000	1895 35,000
1875 75,000	1917 3,000,000	1912 38,500,000	1900 40,000
1876 100,000	1918 3,200,000	1913 40,000,000	1905 50,000
1877 125,000	1919 3,400,000	1914 41,500,000	1910 60,000
1878 150,000	1920 3,600,000	1915 42,500,000	1915 70,000
1879 170,000	1921 3,750,000	1916 45,500,000	1920 75,000
1880 200,000	1922 3,900,000	1917 47,000,000	1925 80,000
1881 220,000	1923 4,000,000	1918 47,500,000	1930 85,000
1882 230,000	1924 4,500,000	1919 50,000,000	1935 90,000
1883 250,000	1925 4,700,000	1920 55,000,000	1940 100,000
1884 285,000	1926 4,800,000	1921 58,000,000	
1885 310,000		1922 60,500,000	

Longines

1867	1
1870	20,000
1880	200,000
1882	250,000
1888	500,000
1890	600,000
1893	750,000
1899	1,000,000
1900	1,200,000
1901	1,250,000
1904	1,500,000
1905	1,750,000
1910	2,000,000
1920	3,000,000
1930	5,000,000
1940	6,000,000

Manhattan

1885	200,000
1895	500,000

Manistee

1910	40,000
1915	60,000

New Haven Clock and Watch Co.

1890	2,000,000
1895	3,000,000
1900	5,000,000
1905	7,000,000
1910	10,000,000
1915	14,000,000
1920	18,000,000
1925	25,000,000
1930	30,000,000

Newark Watch Co.

As Newark Watch Co., 1864-1870 6,901-12,000
As Cornell Watch Co. (Chicago 1870-1874) 12,001-25,000
As Cornell Watch Co. (San Francisco 1874-1876) 25,001-35,000
Ending as the California Watch Co., Jan. 1876-July 1876.

New York Standard

1890	600,000
1895	900,000
1900	1,200,000
1905	1,500,000
1910	1,800,000
1915	2,100,000
1920	2,400,000
1925	2,700,000
1930	3,000,000

Omega (Courtesy of Omega Watch Co.)

1894	1,000,000
1902	2,000,000
1906	3,000,000
1910	4,000,000
1915	5,000,000
1920	6,000,000
1923	7,000,000
1926	8,000,000
1934	9,000,000
1944	10,000,000
1947	11,000,000
1950	12,000,000
1952	13,000,000
1954	14,000,000
1956	15,000,000
1958	16,000,000
1959	17,000,000
1961	18,000,000
1962	19,000,000
1963	20,000,000
1964	21,000,000
1965	22,000,000
1966	23,000,000 -24,000,000
1967	25,000,000
1968	26,000,000 -27,000,000
1969	28,000,000 -31,000,000
1970	32,000,000
1971	33,000,000
1972	34,000,000 -35,000,000
1973	36,000,000 -37,000,000
1974	38,000,000
1975	39,000,000
1977	40,000,000
1978	41,000,000
1979	42,000,000 -43,000,000

Patek Philippe

1845	1,500
1850	4,000
1855	9,000
1860	16,000
1865	25,000
1870	35,000
1875	45,000
1880	55,000
1885	70,000
1890	85,000
1895	100,000
1900	115,000
1905	130,000
1910	170,000
1915	178,000
1920	185,000
1925	200,000

Peoria

1890	50,000
1895	75,000
1900	100,000

Rockford

1876	5,000
1877	15,000
1878	25,000
1879	35,000
1880	50,000
1881	60,000
1882	70,000
1883	80,000
1884	90,000
1885	100,000
1886	110,000
1887	125,000
1888	140,000
1889	150,000
1890	165,000
1891	175,000
1892	195,000
1993	200,000
1894	230,000
1895	260,000
1896	290,000
1897	320,000
1898	350,000

1899 385,000	1949 608,500	1893 200,000	1919 880,000
1900 415,000	1950 673,600	1894 240,000	1920 910,000
1901 450,000	1951 738,700	1895 280,000	1921 930,000
1902 480,000	1952 803,800	1896 330,000	1922 960,000
1903 515,000	1953 868,900	1897 370,000	1923 980,000
1904 550,000	1954 934,000	1898 420,000	1924 1,050,000
1905 580,000	1955 1,012,000	1899 460,000	1925 1,100,000
1906 620,000	1956 1,090,000	1900 500,000	1926 1,150,000
1907 650,000	1957 1,168,000	1901 550,000	1927 1,200,000
1908 690,000	1958 1,246,000	1902 600,000	1928 1,250,000
1909 730,000	1959 1,324,000	1903 650,000	1929 1,300,000
1910 765,000	1960 1,402,000	1904 710,000	
1911 820,000	1961 1,480,000	1905 760,000	**Trenton**
1912 850,000	1962 1,558,000	1906 820,000	1890 150,000
1913 880,000	1963 1,636,000	1907 930,000	1895 500,000
1914 930,000	1964 1,714,000	1908 1,055,000	1900 2,000,000
1915 1,000,000	1965 1,792,000	1909 1,175,000	1905 2,500,000
	1966 1,871,000	1910 1,325,000	1910 3,000,000
Rolex	1967 2,163,900	1911 1,835,000	1915 3,500,000
1926 28,000	1968 2,426,800	1912 2,355,000	1920 4,000,000
1927 30,430	1969 2,689,700	1913 3,000,000	
1928 32,960	1970 2,952,600	1914 3,600,000	**U. S. Marion**
1929 35,390	1971 3,215,500		1870 40,000
1930 37,820	1972 3,478,400	**South Bend**	1875 250,000
1931 40,250	1973 3,741,300	**Watch Co.**	
1932 42,680	1974 4,004,200	1903 300,000	**U.S. Watch Co.**
1934 45,000	1975 4,267,100	1904 335,000	**of Waltham**
1935 63,000	1976 4,539,000	1905 360,000	1887 3,000
1936 81,000	1977 5,006,000	1906 400,000	1888 6,500
1937 99,000	1978 5,482,000	1907 445,000	1889 10,000
1938 117,000	1979 5,958,000	1908 480,000	1890 30,000
1939 135,000		1909 520,000	1891 60,000
1940 164,600	**Seth Thomas**	1910 540,000	1892 90,000
1941 194,200	1885 5,000	1911 590,000	1893 150,000
1942 223,800	1886 10,000	1912 625,000	1894 200,000
1943 253,400	1887 20,000	1913 650,000	1895 250,000
1944 283,000	1888 50,000	1914 700,000	1896 300,000
1945 348,100	1889 80,000	1915 730,000	1897 350,000
1946 413,200	1890 110,000	1916 765,000	1898 400,000
1947 478,300	1891 150,000	1917 800,000	1899 500,000
1948 543,400	1892 175,000	1918 845,000	1900 600,000

1901 700,000	
1902 750,000	
1903 800,000	

Vacheron Constantin

1850 50,000
1890 180,000
1895 217,000
1900 255,000
1905 287,000
1910 330,000
1915 360,000
1920 390,000
1925 398,000
1930 405,000
1935 427,000
1940 450,000
1945 475,000
1950 500,000
1955 525,000
1960 550,000

Waltham (American Watch Co.)

1854 1,000
1857 5,000
1858 10,000
1859 15,000
1860 20,000
1861 25,000
1862 35,000
1863 45,000
1864 110,000
1865 180,000

1866 260,000
1867 330,000
1868 410,000
1869 460,000
1870 500,000
1871 540,000
1872 590,000
1873 680,000
1874 730,000
1875 810,000
1876 910,000
1877 1,000,000
1878 1,150,000
1879 1,350,000
1880 1,500,000
1881 1,670,000
1882 1,835,000
1883 2,000,000
1884 2,350,000
1885 2,650,000
1886 3,000,000
1887 3,400,000
1888 3,800,000
1889 4,200,000
1890 4,700,000
1891 5,200,000
1892 5,800,000
1893 6,300,000
1894 6,700,000
1895 7,100,000
1896 7,450,000
1897 8,100,000
1898 8,400,000
1899 9,000,000
1900 9,500,000
1901 10,200,000

1902 11,100,000
1903 12,100,000
1904 13,500,000
1905 14,300,000
1906 14,700,000
1907 15,500,000
1908 17,000,000
1909 17,600,000
1910 17,900,000
1911 18,100,000
1912 18,200,000
1913 18,900,000
1914 19,500,000
1915 20,000,000
1916 20,500,000
1917 20,900,000
1918 21,800,000
1919 22,500,000
1920 23,400,000
1921 23,900,000
1922 24,100,000
1923 24,300,000
1924 24,500,000
1926 25,200,000
1927 26,100,000
1928 26,400,000
1929 26,900,000
1930 27,100,000
1931 27,300,000
1932 27,550,000
1933 27,750,000
1934 28,100,000
1935 28,600,000
1936 29,100,000
1937 29,400,000
1938 29,750,000

1939 30,050,000
1940 30,250,000
1941 30,750,000
1942 31,050,000
1943 31,400,000
1944 31,700,000
1945 32,100,000
1946 32,350,000
1947 32,750,000
1948 33,100,000
1949 33,500,000
1950 33,560,000
1951 33,600,000
1952 33,700,000
1953 33,800,000
1954 34,100,000
1955 34,450,000
1956 34,700,000
1957 35,000,000

Waterbury

1880 100,000
1885 1,000,000
1890 3,000,000
1895 5,000,000
1900 7,500,000
1905 9,000,000
1910 12,000,000

Westclox

1905 4,000,000
1910 10,000,000
1915 18,000,000
1920 25,000,000
1925 37,000,000
1930 50,000,000